Linda Wommack's latest book, Colorado's Historic Mansions and Castles, *brings Leadville to life and gives great insight to this "City in the Clouds" in its early days. August Meyer's impact on the fledgling city is carefully portrayed, as well as the "little mansion on the hill" he built for his bride, Emma. Linda's attention to detail is evident throughout the chapter, while providing an interesting and informative read. Well done!*

—Maureen Scanlon, Regional Director, Healy House, Leadville, Colorado

This book creates excellent imagery of the fine ladies and gentlemen of Colorado's yesteryear in their elegant homes. Wommack's authentic descriptions and historical knowledge will not only take you back in time but also compel you to visit the mansions in the present.

—Maretta Characky, Coordinator, the Robison Mansion & Carriage House

Interesting and easy to read, Wommack's peek into Colorado's majestic homes will entertain and educate everyone who picks up the book. The stories behind the buildings are brought to life through her detailed and spirited descriptions of the families who lived there, the towns where they were located and the happenings of the time period. If you haven't visited the featured locations, you will want to after reading this book. This treasure of information and narratives would be a wonderful addition to any collection.

—Deb Darrow, Rosemount Museum Executive Director, Pueblo, Colorado

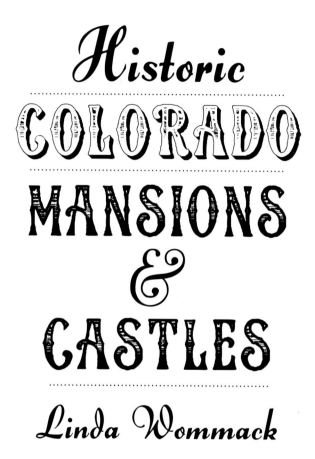

Historic
COLORADO
MANSIONS
&
CASTLES

Linda Wommack

THE
History
PRESS

Published by The History Press
Charleston, SC 29403
www.historypress.net

Copyright © 2014 by Linda Wommack
All rights reserved

First published 2014

Manufactured in the United States

ISBN 978.1.62619.748.0

Library of Congress CIP data applied for.

Dedicated to Connie Clayton
Her passion, professionalism and keen insight greatly enhanced this work.

CONTENTS

ACKNOWLEDGEMENTS

The history of these mansions and castles comes alive with the stories of the men and women who built them. I am indebted to the many owners, curators, directors and managers of these historic properties who gave so freely of their time and knowledge.

Perhaps the most fun in the research process was in talking with these men and women who have such a passion for their work. Their enthusiasm for the history of their landmark establishments was infectious. Peggie Yager, director of the Miramont Castle Museum, generously provided me with open access to the museum archives. Through our tours of the castle, she pointed out several unique and little-known features as well as dispelled some age-old myths. Peggie also graciously read, critiqued and added to the chapter on the fabulous Miramont Castle.

Maretta Characky, Robison Mansion historian, was a pure delight with her knowledge and enthusiasm for this project. She also read and critiqued the Robison chapter. My heartfelt thanks to her for the many contributions and photographs.

Maureen Scanlon, director of the Healy House Museum and Dexter Cabin, was kind enough to not only share her knowledge and sources for much of the historical background for this chapter but also open the museum to me on numerous occasions, and she always had time for my many questions. Her generosity is much appreciated.

James "Jim" Peiker and his daughter, Melissa Feher-Peiker, not only opened the doors of their historic Denver mansion to me, but they also graciously offered their time and freely satisfied my curiosity. Melissa showed me just about every nook and cranny in Castle Marne, and Jim patiently answered my many questions, but provided so much more than I could ever have imagined. With his subsequent historic discoveries since purchasing the mansion, Jim enlightened me to a historic tale that came full circle over a century later. That history is included in this work, told for the first time. I treasure my time with the Peiker family.

As many of these millionaire mansion builders were involved in banking, I found myself relying again and again on my old friend Robert S. Pulcipher, Denver's banking historian. Pulcipher not only clarified individual situations, but he also added important details to the narrative, some of which are included, and some of which, well, aren't.

To assemble the historic photographs, I relied on the fabulous work of friend Coi E. Drummond-Gerhig, digital image collection administrator for the Denver Public Library. This was a vital aspect of the content of the book, as photos of both the residences and the people who built them are the essence of the narrative.

Special thanks go to those who believed in this project and gave freely of their time and advice. First on that list is my husband, Frank, who tolerated the many late nights of research and writing and helped to work out the research obstacles. To my dear friend Connie Clayton, who diligently edited the manuscript with wit and humor and became my support line on many levels, my sincere thanks.

To all of you, my heartfelt thanks.

—Linda Wommack, July 20, 2014

INTRODUCTION

Mansions and even castles—for Colorado does boast a few of these structures—were not only a symbol of wealth and prominence but also added a sense of refinement to the growing towns and cities of Colorado.

In the years following the Pikes Peak gold rush of 1859, a steady stream of gold-seekers and entrepreneurs traveled to the region, most heading toward Denver City and on to the mountain mining camps.

A few of these men and women remained in the cities or built new cities. They were the businessmen, town leaders, politicians and industrialists who would help build and promote the region. Included were men such as William Newton Byers, who wrote one of the many emigrant guidebooks promoting the area and advising prospective settlers on the best routes to Denver and the gold fields. Byers would further his cause through the pages of his *Rocky Mountain News*, established in April 1859. With Byers's tireless promotion, Colorado statehood was achieved in August 1876.

Colorado's early businessmen found wealth by investing in Colorado's mining industry. August A. Meyer and Lyman Robison, who both made millions from Leadville's silver riches, are two such men. James Joseph Brown, a Leadville mining superintendent, improved the production and received $1 million in stockholder dividends for his efforts. He and his wife, Margaret Tobin Brown, would buy what would become Denver's most famous mansion, the House of Lions.

Walter Scott Cheesman, a druggist by trade, came to Denver City in July 1861. He would go on to improve Denver's quality of living with his Denver

Gas Company and the city's water supply, eventually building the Cheesman Dam. His stately mansion in Denver's Capitol Hill neighborhood would later be home to the governors of Colorado.

Scandal and even murder surround these palatial pioneer palaces. Isabel Springer, for whom Castle Isabel was named, became the center of attention in the state's most sensational murder trial. Father Jean Baptiste Francolon, who built the eclectic Miramont Castle, received his share of scandalous accusations and rumors.

The lives of these men and women who built these mansions are revealed in detail, as are the now historic dwellings that they called "home."

These landmark castles and mansions have achieved listings on one, if not all, categories of preservation status, including: 1) National Register of Historic Places, 2) National Trust for Historic Preservation, 3) Colorado Preservation, Inc., as "landmark" status, or 4) listed with city or county historic properties.

There are many homes across the state that have received historic preservation status. A very important distinction with this work is that these residences included are actually open to the public.

Early on in my research, I wrestled with the question, "What constitutes a mansion?" I learned there are no easy answers. Architectural historians differ as to time period or era of construction, such as Roman-Renaissance-Baroque architecture, introduced in America in 1850; early French Renaissance style, introduced in 1870; or Italian Renaissance Revival, revived in early nineteenth-century American structures. In short, as men and women prospered over time, their homes also reflected the architectural designs of the era.

The U.S. Real Estate Association defines a mansion as "a dwelling of over 8,000 square feet. A traditional European mansion was defined as a house which contained a ballroom and many bedrooms. Today, however, there is no formal definition beyond being a large and well-appointed house."

Using this definition, as well as the qualifier of being open to the public, helped define the subject matter. While the original construction of a few of the residences was well under the eight-thousand-square-feet "rule," with remodeling and additions, the homes did eventually become mansions. Surprisingly, the only exception is the Molly Brown House, which falls short by a mere eighty-one square feet.

Throughout the chapters, readers will discover the many family connections. For instance, William Gray Evans, the second owner of the Byers-Evans House, was the son of Colorado territorial governor

John Evans. John Evans II married Gladys Cheesman and lived in the Cheesman-Evans-Boettcher mansion.

These stories reflect the history of these landmark homes and the personalities and lives of the men and women who built them.

Chapter 1

HEALY HOUSE—LEADVILLE—1878

THE HOUSE ON THE HILL

The Beginning

With the discovery of gold in 1858, mining became Colorado's economic backbone, eventually leading to statehood in 1876. The rush of miners, tenderfeet, merchants and fortune seekers who headed west during the Pikes Peak gold rush of 1858–59 were known as '59ers. These pioneers, through their political leadership and business foresight, built and shaped the territory that would become the state of Colorado. Through the direct cause and effect of the gold frenzy, mining became the foremost industry in the state. Rich strikes occurred all over the state, from Central City to the San Juan mountain range and from Creede to Leadville.

It was William H. Stevens who actually led the first group of miners up the Rocky Mountains to a place where the first silver riches would eventually be found. It was Stevens who would figure out that the dark, dingy, slimy mud miners had to separate from the gold was actually a carbonate of silver. But that would be fifteen years in the future. Meanwhile, in the spring of 1860, Stevens and his group, which included Abe Lee, followed Bear Creek to the South Platte River and then headed west through the South Park region, where they crossed the Mosquito Range at some point near the present town of Granite. By April 1860, they had located the Arkansas River, which led them to the valley and dry gulches between Colorado's highest peaks: Mount Elbert, at 14,433 feet, and Mount Massive, at 14,421 feet. They followed a promising stream, yielding "color," near a gulch crowded between Carbonate Hill and Rock Hill to the west. Abe Lee pulled out a sample of gold from his pan and exclaimed, "Boys, I've got all of California in this here pan."

With Abe Lee's find, the area was called California Gulch. Miners swarmed to the area, and soon the mining camp of Oro City was established. One of those miners was Horace A.W. Tabor. A tried and true '59er, Tabor brought his wife, Augusta, and infant son, Maxcy, to the gold riches of the Colorado Rockies following the original Gregory strike. After a few attempts at gold mining, particularly at Payne's Bar (Idaho Springs), where his claim was jumped, the Tabors moved up the hills, finally arriving in the Oro City settlement, such as it was, in the fall of 1860. While Tabor immediately set out prospecting in the area, Augusta saw the advantage of business opportunities and opened a baking shop. So popular were her baked goods—and perhaps because she was the only woman in the camp—that the miners built her a cabin, where she could expand her cooking skills for all the men. Here the Tabor family stayed and helped build the community. Later, Augusta became postmistress, and Tabor was elected mayor.

In 1870, activity in the region picked up when William Stevens and Alvinus B. Wood constructed a water pipeline in the gulch about a mile below Oro City. They were convinced that the gold in the area had to be washed out by an extensive placer mining method. After spending over $50,000 building the water pipeline, their operation succeeded. However, the heavy black soil still slowed the process and became quite a nuisance. Curious, Stevens packed up a few soil samples from the bedrock and the stream underlay and headed for the local assayer. Incredibly, the black sludge was discovered to be a carbonate of lead, the parent rock of silver! Those few small samples that Stevens brought in assayed at two and a half pounds of silver to the ton.

In 1876, the very year Colorado became a state, a new rush to the Rocky Mountains was on. Silver! The entire area swarmed almost overnight with miners in a frenzy to strike it rich. Before the year was out, $100,000 worth of silver came out of the first developed mine in California Gulch, and a year later, a new town would be incorporated closer to the major mining claims. It would be named Leadville.

Among one of the many men who arrived in Oro City during the early days of the silver rush was August R. Meyer. Meyer had accepted the position of territorial assayer in the district of Fairplay in 1874. His credentials for such a position were quite impressive.

Meyer, born in St. Louis, Missouri, in 1851, was sent to Switzerland at the age of fourteen to study metallurgy, geology and chemistry at the Cantonal College of Zurich. From there, he continued his studies at the school of mines in Freilberg, Saxony. He later completed his education at the University of Berlin, earning a degree in mining engineering. Meyer returned to St. Louis in 1873, where he worked for a year before accepting the Colorado offer of employment. During his time in Fairplay, Meyer was instrumental in the construction of the first sampling works in Alma. The company, the St. Louis Smelting and Refining Company, would later play an important part in Meyer's financial success.

Meyer arrived in Oro City in August 1876 to examine the mining operations and report his findings to the territorial assayer office. Meyer saw the economic potential of the carbonate ore and purchased the first recorded ore claim in September 1876. He loaded the rich ore into a wagon and drove the oxen wagon to the railroad in Colorado Springs. Here the ore was assayed at a high rate. In the spring of 1877, Meyer filed an additional mining claim, which he named the Pinnacle. At the same time, Meyer established a sampling mill in lower Oro City, sending shipments of ore to the St. Louis Smelting and Refining Company.

In early 1877, Meyer was hired by Edwin Harrison, president of the St. Louis Smelting and Refining Company, to keep the company informed on the progress of the ore discoveries in the new "carbonate camp" of Oro City. With the rich silver lodes, Meyer's company provided the financial backing for him to build the August R. Meyer Ore Milling & Sampling Company to ship the rich ore. Meyer's company was responsible for building roads that led directly to the mining camp of Oro City. This allowed him to organize a regular freighting system to get supplies into the mining camp and the ore to the assaying and processing facilities, charging local merchants a discounted rate. Meyer's company also handled the banking needs of Oro City. Meyer became known as "the father of the carbonate camp."

However, to reduce the metal ore to molten metal or slags, thereby providing a more profitable means for shipping, a smelter in the area was greatly needed. In June 1877, the president of the St. Louis Smelting and Refining Company, Edwin Harrison, personally visited the area. Harrison, a mining man with experience and knowledge, spent considerable time looking over the area, noting all the logistics and details. With a satisfying assessment, Harrison agreed to build a smelter. A month later, the St. Louis Smelting and Refining Company began erecting the smelter about two miles northwest of Oro City. The offices were built at what became the corner of Chestnut Street and Harrison Avenue, in the new town of Leadville.

With the completion of the new smelter operation in October 1877, Meyer then hired men to improve the roads to the mines in both the California and Stray Horse gulches and over Weston Pass for transporting the ore and equipment to the railroads in Canon City and Colorado Springs. Meyer hired sixteen teams of oxen to haul the refined product from the smelter over the mountains to the eastbound railroad lines. James B. Grant, who would later become governor of Colorado, also had mining interests in the area. He purchased a team of mules to haul his ore and coke over Meyer's new roadway.

By the close of 1877, Lake County, one of the original counties created when Colorado became a territory in 1861, ranked fourth among the state's mineral producing counties. A year later, it was ranked first in the state. August R. Meyer figured highly in the state's report as the number-one shipper of ore in the county, shipping over eight thousand tons of ore valued at $1,162,559.39. Incredibly, the following year, Meyer's silver ore doubled in value to $2,702,929.60.

Processing and delivering the ore was now simplified. The advent of this refining process, more than any other, caused the early businessmen of Oro City, such as H.A.W. Tabor and August Meyer, among others, to permanently move to the new site soon to be known as Leadville. Years later, in an interview with the *Herald Democrat* newspaper, published in 1891, Alvinus B. Wood recalled:

> *It was on the last day of April when I found a lead of carbonate ore cropping out on either side of California gulch. I knew what it was and followed the float for nearly two miles to a place under the porphyry and in the limestone. I did not say anything to anyone. August R. Meyer, now president of the Arkansas Valley smelter, and who then was an ore buyer, after seeing the returns of 60 per cent [sic] lead and 10 to 12 ounces of silver showing up from every hole on the six claims, agreed to take the ore and ship it to the nearest smelter which was in St. Louis. It was he who bought the New Mexico bull teams and hauled the ore to Canon City and Colorado Springs and from there it was shipped by rail to its destination.*

In the summer of 1878, Leadville, known as the "City above the Clouds," was incorporated. At an elevation of 10,152 feet, Leadville became the highest city in America.

Meyer, along with George L. Henderson and Alvinus B. Wood, platted the streets of the new mining town. Chestnut Street, bustling with over one hundred businesses, became the main commercial street. Harrison Avenue, named in honor of Edwin Harrison, ran south to the many smelting operations.

By the following spring of 1879, Leadville's population was exploding. As more people arrived and businesses were clamoring for lots, Harrison Avenue soon became the commercial street in town, overtaking the once busy Chestnut Street. Lots on Harrison Avenue that were offered the previous year for $200 were now sold for over $5,000. The town fathers improved the appeal of Harrison Avenue, and a post office was established, operated by the Tabors.

Leadville's *Herald Democrat* newspaper dated January 1, 1883, printed an account of an interview with Meyer, who recalled the January 14, 1878 meeting when the discussion of the town's name was the main topic:

George L. Henderson, Miss Lottie Williams, Alvinus B. Wood and Aug. R. Meyer met by appointment in Henderson's cabin to agree upon a name to be incorporated in a petition about to be forwarded to the second assistant postmaster general, requesting that official to establish a post office in this locality. Four names were suggested and discussed, Carbonate, Cerrusite, Meyer and Leadville—and the latter was finally selected and recommended in the petition which also solicited the appointment of H.A.W. Tabor as postmaster. Mr. Wood had suggested Lead City, but it was agreed that it could be confused with a town of the same name in the Black Hills. Leadville was accepted as a compromise.

On April 10, 1882, Meyer and a group of Leadville businessmen, including H.A.W. Tabor, entered into an agreement to form the Arkansas Valley Smelting Company. By June, articles of incorporation were filed with $500,000 in capital stock. The largest stockholder was Meyer, who also became the first elected to the board of directors as vice-president. He would later become president. With Meyer's financial success secured, his future was about to become even brighter.

Glory Days

In early 1878, Meyer was introduced to twenty-year-old Emily "Emma" Jane Hixon. Miss Hixon worked as a postmistress in Tabor's Leadville post office. Emma was the oldest of eleven children who had arrived in Denver with their parents, John and Margaret Hixon, by train from Missouri in 1877. Their train trip into the city was anything but normal. As the train rolled toward Union Station, traveling too fast, the train jumped the tracks, crashing into a warehouse. The Hixon family, unhurt, eventually found work and accommodations on a farm near Cherry Creek. Emma gained employment at a Denver coffee-packing warehouse. In August of that year, Emma left Denver, her family and friends and set out for Leadville, eventually securing the position at Tabor's post office.

The attraction between Meyer and Miss Hixon was immediate, and the courtship was brief. On May 24, 1878, August R. Meyer and Emily "Emma" Jane Hixon were united in marriage in the home of H.A.W. Tabor and his wife, Augusta. Officiating the ceremony was Joseph Adams. Witnesses were Tabor and Mr. M.L. Clark.

Just a few weeks after the wedding, during the summer months of 1878, Meyer began building a new home for his bride. He picked the perfect spot on the high hill at the north end of Harrison Avenue, overlooking the city below, yet high enough and away from the pollution of smelters, including his own.

The two-story Greek Revival white clapboard home was the finest home in Leadville. The exterior was resplendent with ornate features, such as large windows with painted shutters. The shingled hip roof included two chimneys.

The home faced west with a spectacular view of the mountains. The Harrison Street side of the property featured a stone border. Above the surrounding street-side stone border, a lovely white-painted picket fence surrounded the property. Behind the home was an outhouse, as well as a barn and stables for the horses. A stone-stepped stairway led from the street to the inviting porch entrance at the west side of the home.

The entrance to the Meyer home was enhanced with an Italianate bracketed and balustraded porch. The balcony on the second floor, directly above the porch entrance, featured the same Italianate bracketed wooden fencing and offered an elevated commanding view of the Rocky Mountains. A large garden at the south end of the Meyer property completed the grounds, allowing for a pleasant overview of the bustling cloud city below. It was soon known by Leadville citizens as the "little mansion on the hill."

When the residence was completed in early 1879, the Meyers moved into a luxurious home, adorned in the finest of Victorian decorations and furniture. With nine rooms in total, the Meyer home included a formal parlor, dining room and kitchen on the first floor. The parlor, with a large fireplace, featured a mantle in a faux finish, designed with a feather to resemble a marble texture. The fireplace screen included the Colorado state seal, embroidered in silk. The formal dining room boasted a magnificent black oak sideboard. Meyer had it made in Germany and shipped to America. On the last leg of the journey to Leadville, the sideboard fell off the wagon on the rough road over Mosquito Pass, cracking the beautiful marble top. Nevertheless, the Meyers proudly placed it in the dining room.

The library on this floor also served as August Meyer's smoking room, where he entertained his gentlemen guests following dinner.

There was no indoor plumbing, so water was obtained by a pump in the kitchen. This was also the room where the Meyers took their baths in a galvanized folding bathtub, complete with a privacy screen.

The center hall led to a steep and narrow oak staircase leading to the bedrooms on the second floor. There were five bedrooms on this floor.

The Meyers lived in the home for three years. He and his wife, Emma, often held social and political gatherings in their home. During this time, Meyer kept active with his various business interests. Emma Meyer was quite involved in the community in various church and social activities.

In 1882, Meyer had accepted a position with his former St. Louis employers. He sold the home and returned to Missouri. He and Emma would eventually have seven children. August R. Meyer died December 1, 1905. Emily "Emma" Jane Hixon Meyer died January 3, 1932. Both are buried in the Elwood cemetery in Kansas City, Missouri.

The Meyer home was bought by Leadville's Methodist Episcopal Church for $4,000. For the next four years, the house served as the parsonage and social hall for the church.

And the Rest Is History

On June 15, 1886, Patrick A. and Ellen Healy Kelly bought the home from the Methodist Episcopal Church for fifteen hundred dollars, as a business investment. Patrick Kelly was well established in Leadville. He had been the former town marshal of Leadville, having defeated the infamous Martin Duggan in a four to one vote by the Leadville City council. When he met and later married Ellen Healy, Kelly was a highly respected member of Leadville's business community.

Ellen's father, Maytor J. Healy, had immigrated to America for a better life for his large family. When he had secured work at a smelting plant in Michigan, he sent money to his wife, Nelle Donovan Healy, for passage to America. Young Ellen, along with her mother; her sisters, Mary, Julia and Brenda; and brothers, Patrick and Daniel, left County Kerry, Ireland, in 1862, arriving at the Port of New York on October 8, 1862. From there, they made their way to Hancock, Michigan, where they were greeted by the children's father.

Ellen arrived in Leadville in 1878. After her marriage to Patrick Kelly, the couple was soon blessed with three children.

The Kellys operated the former Meyer home as a boardinghouse, which soon became quite popular. It became known as the "Kelly House on the Hill," although the Kelly family did not live in the house. Boarders, from schoolteachers to railroad workers, flocked to the house. For years, it was a sought-after boardinghouse and the hub of social life for many of the working class. Added attractions included croquet on the lawn.

In 1885, Ellen's younger brother, twenty-five-year-old Daniel Healy, arrived in Leadville after receiving a letter of invitation from his sister Ellen. Healy had attended school in Hancock, Michigan, while also working, at the age of nine, with his older sister's husband, Bernard Hoppenyan, at his copper smelting company, known as the Workhouse. As he grew older, Daniel attended the Northern Indiana Normal School, in Valparaiso, Indiana. Following his graduation, he became a schoolteacher in Marquette, Michigan.

Arriving in Leadville, Healy immediately went to work helping his sister and her husband in the boardinghouse operations, while also looking for additional work. In 1887, Healy obtained a position as mail carrier for the Leadville post office. Two years later, he was promoted to assistant postmaster. After six years, he left this position and entered into the insurance and real estate business. His new business enterprises became quite successful. Even so, Healy continued to live in the boardinghouse high on the hill.

In early 1895, with Ellen pregnant with their fourth child, the Kelly family moved into the "Kelly House." Tragically, on May 25, 1895, Ellen Healy Kelly died in childbirth. Sadly, the child, Patrick Albert Kelly, also died. Two days later, Patrick Kelly buried his beloved wife and infant son in Leadville's Evergreen Cemetery.

A grieving and forlorn Patrick Kelly sold the former Meyer home to his brother-in-law, Daniel Healy. Healy immediately sent a request to his cousin Nellie A. Healy to join him in Leadville and help in the operation of the boardinghouse. Daniel knew of his cousin's health issues and thought that the high altitude would improve her condition.

Both Nellie and Daniel's fathers had emigrated together from Ireland to America. However, Nellie's father was a widower, and young Nellie spent most of her youth in a Catholic convent in Quebec, Canada. Completing her formal education, Nellie earned a teaching certificate and taught school until she received the invitation from her cousin Daniel to come west to Leadville.

Nellie joined her cousin Daniel in 1895, working in the day-to-day operations of the boardinghouse. Meanwhile, Daniel made improvements to the home. To expand the small kitchen, Healy had the barn moved and attached to the original kitchen at the southeast end of the original home, in an effort to provide a larger area for the needs of the boarders. He also installed indoor plumbing, a luxury that was available in Leadville by 1886. The upper rooms of the barn addition served as quarters for the hired help. He then constructed a third floor to the home, adding five more rooms for boarders. He hired Mr. and Mrs. Harper to manage the operations of the boardinghouse when Nellie secured a teaching position in the Leadville school district, teaching fifth-grade students at the Sinth Street School.

As Nellie became more involved in Leadville society, she suggested that the Harpers rent the third floor rooms primarily to schoolteachers. Several teachers lived in the boardinghouse, as it was fairly affordable at thirty dollars a month, which included meals.

With the boardinghouse in firm hands, Daniel Healy entered politics. He was elected state senator by the Democratic party in 1903, for the Sixteenth Congressional District, which included Leadville.

While on a fishing trip at nearby Turquoise Lake, Daniel Healy drowned in a tragic event on May 20, 1912. The *Leadville Democrat* carried his obituary, stating in part: "Daniel Healy drowned in the shallows of Turquoise Lake after suffering an epileptic seizure."

Daniel's funeral was held in the formal parlor of the Healy home on May 25, 1912. Among the large group of mourners in attendance were his brothers Patrick and Maytor James, sisters Julia Young and Mrs. Mary Hoppenyan and Nellie A. Healy. Burial followed in the Catholic section of the Evergreen Cemetery.

As Daniel Healy never married, his will left the bulk of his considerable estate to his cousin Nellie Healy. She inherited his insurance and real estate business, as well as the Healy home. Nellie continued to live in the home, while personally operating the boardinghouse. Giving up her teaching position, she also ran the two inherited businesses.

The dining room of the Healy House is set with Victorian-era china. *Linda Wommack.*

Nellie Healy's bed is graced with a doll and her personal Bible. *Linda Wommack.*

Nellie Healy was very active in community affairs. During World War I, she hosted dances and charity events in the dining room of her home. Following the war, Healy's various businesses remained viable until the Great Depression of the 1930s. At the height of the Depression years, she was the only resident in the boardinghouse. During the winter months she lived in Ogden, Utah. Without continued maintenance, the house soon fell into disrepair.

In 1936, Nellie Healy met with Marian P. "Poppy" Smith, the head of the Leadville Historical Society, and Clara Gaw. During the meeting, she gave Smith a set of encyclopedias. At the end of the meeting, she handed over the keys to the historic home. Thus, Nellie Healy donated her inherited home and the furnishings to the Leadville Historical Society.

The historical society, with limited funds, did the necessary repairs to ensure the home was structurally sound. The Ladies of the Leadville Association, again led by Poppy Smith, were largely responsible for the restoration process. The home was then opened to the public as the Healy House Museum, with Poppy Smith as the resident curator. However, the museum struggled during World War II. Following the war, with not enough funds to continue operation and maintenance, the Leadville Historical Society deeded the Healy House museum to the Colorado Historical Society in 1947.

Today

August R. Meyer's 1878 Greek Revival clapboard home is the oldest home of its size and stature in Leadville. Today it is a museum open to the public known as the Healy House Museum. The home has been beautifully restored and features lavish Victorian furnishings collected by Leadville citizens, including light fixtures, furniture, musical instruments and personal possessions once owned by Horace and Augusta Tabor. From the front entrance of the home, where the original oil lamp remains where Meyer installed it, visitors are treated to examples of Victorian life in a mountain mining community.

The grounds feature the formal garden with several native plants, Victorian urns, statuary, garden benches and a gazebo. The restored gardens at the south end of the home, named in honor of Emma Meyer, the first lady of the historic home, include heirloom and native plants. A white-framed gazebo, at the south end of the garden, allows visitors a wonderful view of the scenic

Leadville's Healy House was built high on a hill in 1878. *Elkman Photography.*

beauty of Colorado's highest mountains, Mount Elbert and Mount Massive, as well as a grand view of the storied mining town below that is Leadville.

Fun Facts

- The galvanized bathtub, believed to be original to the home and which folded up to the wall, was manufactured by the Mosley Water Tub Company and is a unique feature in the museum.
- The German-made black oak sideboard still commands its original spot in the formal dining room. This sideboard along with a large bed on the second floor are the only pieces of furniture once owned by the Meyers in the Healy House Museum today.
- A large beautiful signature quilt hangs on a wall in the Healy House. It is undated but bears the signature of August R. Meyer, stitched in gold-colored thread. As Meyer left Leadville for Kansas in 1882, it obviously

was made prior to that date. Many early and prominent Leadville citizens' signatures are on the quilt. Curiously enough, the signature of H.A.W. Tabor is not.

- A large, vertical, diamond-dust pier mirror was later placed in the formal parlor. Located between the two windows in the room, it also allowed for additional light.
- The cook for the boardinghouse during Daniel Healy's ownership was Julia Martin, who had emigrated from Norway in 1891. She and her husband lived on Chicken Hill, just east of the city on East Third Street. Following the death of her husband, she found work at Healy's boardinghouse. She often claimed she had to walk uphill both ways to reach work and home.
- As a teacher in the Leadville School District, Nellie Healy made approximately $600 a year.
- The only known possessions of Nellie Healy that remain in the home are her Bible, a watercolor painting that hangs in the upper nursery room and a charcoal sketch drawn by her during her days in the Catholic convent.
- The first train to arrive in Leadville was the narrow-gauge Denver and Rio Grande in July 1880.
- Leadville is the highest incorporated city in America at 10,152 feet. The city was so cold in the winter of 1895 that the Ice Palace, a structure made entirely of 8-foot-thick ice blocks, was built as a tourist attraction at a cost of over $200,000. It was a lot of money to spend in those days only to have it melt away with the spring thaw. Before it melted away, ironically in one of the warmest spring thaws in Leadville history, the Ice Palace covered five acres, contained huge ice statues and was the scene of various balls and special events.
- The Healy House was placed on the National Register of Historic Places on June 28, 1971, ILK.4.

Contact Information

HEALY HOUSE MUSEUM
912 Harrison Avenue, Leadville, Colorado 80461
www.historycolorado.org
(719) 486-0487

Chapter 2
BYERS-EVANS HOUSE—DENVER—1883

DENVER'S OLDEST MANSION

Downtown Denver is a bustling business center filled with skyscraper buildings that shadow the sidewalks and halt the wind. It is a stark contrast to the dry, wind-blown prairie of 1859, when Denver City began as a simple supply town to the rich gold fields of the Rocky Mountains.

Tucked away in the midst of these tall financial buildings is a much smaller dwelling, yet it is just as important to the city of Denver, for it was the home of two of the most important and influential pioneer families in Denver history.

The Beginning

The discovery of gold in Colorado in 1858 brought a deluge of determined and eager fortune-seeking Easterners west in the spring of 1859. This new wave of westward adventurers captured the slogan "Pikes Peak or Bust." Many members of this group stayed in the rough mining-supply camp at the confluence of the South Platte River and Cherry Creek and slowly built the area into a fine little town in the Platte Valley. The founders called it Denver City.

One member of that group would become a staunch supporter of the city and help lead the fight for statehood nearly two decades later. He was William Newton Byers. To accomplish the many goals he envisioned, he had at his disposal a very useful tool that few others had: his own newspaper.

A native of Ohio, at the age of twenty-one, Byers joined a survey party along the Missouri River in 1852. With his newfound experience, he next joined a group headed to Oregon, crossing the Plains along the Platte River in what would become the northeast section of Colorado.

Returning to Ohio in 1853, Byers met the lovely Elizabeth Sumner. Miss Sumner came from a family of politicians. Her maternal grandfather was a governor in the state of Ohio, as well as the last territorial governor and the first state governor of Iowa.

Following a brief courtship, William Newton Byers and Elizabeth Sumner married in West Liberty, Ohio, on November 16, 1854. The newlyweds moved to Omaha City, a newly established town site in Nebraska Territory. There, Byers worked vigorously to incorporate the town and was elected as a city alderman. Later, he was elected to the Legislative Assembly of the Nebraska Territory, serving during the term of 1854–55. William and Elizabeth Byers lived in the fifth house to be built in the growing town where their two children were born: Frank, in 1856, and Mary, in 1858.

During the long winter of 1858–59, Byers, having read of the great gold strike in the Rocky Mountains, resolved to join the Pikes Peak movement to the West as soon as possible. However, a gunshot wound prevented Byers from leaving with the earliest group of spring travelers in 1859.

Restless with anticipation of the coming adventure and wild with ideas, young Byers wrote what would become one of the first guidebooks for the Rocky Mountain region. The pamphlets were printed in Omaha, and the publication received wide circulation and promoted the West far beyond anyone's imagination. Byers had much advice for the traveler, ranging from lists of what to bring west and what not to bring. For example, he wrote:

> *Your ruffled shirts, standing collars and all kinds of fine clothing had better be left in your trunk, or wardrobe at home. Discard all cotton or linen clothing; adapt yourself at once to woolen and leather; provide yourself with woolen underclothes; woolen overshirts, thick and strong and woolen pants. You may also leave your razor, for you won't use it. Pack all your baggage in a carpet or canvas [sic] sack; carry no trunks or boxes, if you can avoid it.*

William Newton Byers, at the age of twenty-eight, was finally able to begin his journey west, joining the second group of gold seekers leaving Omaha late in the spring of 1859. In March of that year, Byers began his forty-two-day journey to the Rocky Mountain West. Also in this group were two friends, Thomas Gibson and John L. Dailey, an experienced printer.

William N. Byers built one of Denver's finest mansions in lower Denver. Today it is Denver's oldest mansion. *Denver Public Library.*

Elizabeth Byers fought for women's rights in early Denver. *Denver Public Library.*

Included in the wagonload of necessities were a used printing press, ink and various printing supplies. Not knowing the first thing about printing, much less news publishing, nevertheless Byers intended to strike gold—not in the gold mines of the Colorado Rockies but in the printed word.

It was a slow trek west across the snow-swept eastern plains. Byers and his group arrived on the banks of Cherry Creek in the Auraria settlement on April 20, 1859. Denver City lay on the opposite bank. This would soon prove to be the first in many of Byers's crusades in the interest of town leadership. Byers took immediate boarding above Richens Lacy "Uncle Dick" Wootton's "business block," the first official business establishment in Denver City.

In April 1859, as the spring thaw gave way to warm weather in the foothills of the Rockies, prospectors and greenhorns headed for the hills in Gregory Gulch. Meanwhile, in Denver City, a contest just as competitive as the rush to the gold diggings began in earnest. As soon as Byers had secured lodging above Wootton's saloon, he set to work the very next day printing his newspaper, which he named the *Rocky Mountain News*.

Having the first printed newspaper in a new development meant control of journalism and the power of the written word in ideas and idealism. John Merrick had arrived in Denver City a few days before Byers and, shortly thereafter, set up his own printing press. Gathering stories and writing articles, his intended publication would be called the *Cherry Creek Pioneer*. The citizens of both Denver City and Auraria watched with great enthusiasm as the exciting race between the publications progressed. The scheduled date was Saturday, April 23, a mere three days after Byers had arrived in the new settlement. Luck and a bit of ingenuity was on Byers's side, for he had already typeset the two inner pages of his paper prior to his arrival. All he needed was a front-page headline and story. Saturday, April 23, 1859, arrived with a powerful snowstorm. Each racing to get his paper out first, Merrick and Byers may well have reinvented the journalism term "getting the scoop." In the end, Byers had his *Rocky Mountain News* on the street a full twenty minutes before Merrick's *Cherry Creek Pioneer* hit the street. Citizens declared the *News* the winner, and Byers achieved his journalistic hold in the infant city. Merrick folded his *Cherry Creek Pioneer* the next day. Years later, Byers described the event: "Merrick brought the first printing press outfit, arriving before I. But the jolly fellow that he was waited to get acquainted before settling into work. Not until I started setting the *News*, did Merrick get busy and the race began."

The front page of that historic first edition of the *Rocky Mountain News* included local and national stories, as well as several ads for local businesses in the left column. Byers's first editorial was more of a greeting to his readers,

The front page of the historic *Rocky Mountain News*, April 1864. *Denver Public Library.*

who would soon learn much more from the new editor. He wrote, "Fondly looking forward to a long and pleasant acquaintance with our readers, hoping well to act our part, we send forth to the world the first number of the *Rocky Mountain News.*"

Byers built his *Rocky Mountain News* building in the creek bed of Cherry Creek. It was swept away by the roaring flood of 1864. *Denver Public Library.*

On page three of the issue, editor Byers wrote of the newspaper race: "Quick Work. On the 21st, at 7 p.m., the wagons carrying our press were driven to the door and we began unloading. We set up our press, arranged our matter, and the next day at 10 p.m. began printing the outside of our first issue."

When Elizabeth Byers arrived in Denver City later that spring with their two small children, Mollie and Frank, W.N. Byers had already secured accommodations for his family. It was a small log cabin, crudely built. Later, the Byers family moved into a larger framed house located behind Wootton's saloon, housing Byers's newspaper office. The offices of the *Rocky Mountain News* moved across Cherry Creek to Denver City on October 15, 1859, when Wootton sold his building. Byers would move the offices again, finally building a fine two-story framed building, curiously enough, on wooden stilts, over the bed of Cherry Creek, in June 1860. He announced the move in his paper, stating: "Our new office is in a large frame building in the middle of Cherry Creek under the sign of the American flag. All arrivals are invited to call and register."

Little did he know that a group of angry men would soon take him up on this invitation.

It was also at this time that Byers began publishing the paper daily, rather than weekly. Byers was a visionary who realized the unlimited opportunity that Colorado had to offer. He promoted that idea, tempered with wisdom and sound judgment in his pages of the *Rocky Mountain News*. Through his positive promotion, he soon gained the attention of the second territorial governor, John Evans. Byers and Evans became lifelong friends. The two men, along with their wives, Elizabeth Byers and Margaret Evans, played pivotal roles in Denver's early growth, establishing a variety of educational, religious and social institutions. Elizabeth Byers and Margaret Evans enrolled their children in the first schools of Denver and also became involved in charity work.

The pages of the *Rocky Mountain News* became Byers's soapbox for everything from social issues, crime and politics to his favorite topic: promoting the Rocky Mountain region. His editorials could wax poetic, seem prophetic at times, scream with the wrath of anger and outrage or sing with praise, depending on the topic. His editorials cut to the edge but always stood for what he believed was right for the new Colorado Territory, created in 1861. It was a courageous position, as not all citizens agreed with him. He survived a flood, death threats, kidnapping and bribing, all the while striving for a better community.

One of the more harrowing events occurred just months after the first publication of Byers's newspaper. It was a series of events that would first cause Byers and Denver City's most notable gambler and saloonkeeper to become allies. Later events would cause friction between the two, only to be resolved by a grateful William N. Byers.

From the day that he rode into Denver City in 1859 and opened a monte game at the Denver House, Charles Harrison became the undisputed leader of Denver's first gambling element. He was a clever and fearless gambler, and those who tried his game learned from their losses early on, yet gained a respect for Charles Harrison. Harrison was a born leader, and he stood in stark contrast to the roughs and "bummers" of the gambling element, a group Byers often editorialized against. Gene Teats, the son of the man who bought the Denver House from Harrison (renaming it the Elephant Corral), later recounted for historians that during the two years Harrison was in Denver City, he shot three men and hanged one. These episodes were well documented in the pages of the *Rocky Mountain News*. However, in July 1860, Byers, the outspoken editor of the paper, and Harrison would find themselves linked together as major figures in a controversy that would bring Denver City to the verge of anarchy.

On July 12, Harrison became involved in an altercation at the Cibola Hall that led to words between Harrison and a gambler named Stark. When Stark pulled a knife, Harrison shouted for the man to put it down. Stark lunged with the knife toward Harrison, and Harrison fired his pistol. Stark later died, an inquest was held and Charley Harrison was cleared and the shooting declared an act of self-defense. William Byers lamented the judicial process in his editorial the following day, writing, "From the facts learned since the shooting, we are led to believe the act was unprovoked, in short, cold-blooded murder."

The editorial hit an already shaky nerve given the evident criminal atmosphere. However, Byers had not only underestimated the evolving business element of Larimer Street, but he apparently had no idea of Harrison's strong influence. The gambler and business owner had gained a well-earned reputation as an honest and fair business operator. In fact, he worked with the local law officials in ridding the city of the corruption of the gaming establishments, also gaining the respect and influence of the local politicians.

Meanwhile, as the day turned to evening, an angry mob formed. When Harrison finally made an appearance, the crowd cheered. Amazement turned to disbelief as Harrison, along with Judge Waggoner, walked past the crowd and toward the office of the newspaper editor, W.N. Byers. The meeting lasted a few hours, with the judge presenting evidence and witnesses to show the facts of the Stark shooting in direct contradiction to the statements made by Byers in his paper. Waggoner further argued that in an honest effort to placate the angry citizens, Byers should issue a public apology.

Harrison, the target of Byers's editorial, emerged from the meeting and immediately calmed the angry mob. For Byers's part, with the evidence presented, as well as the mounting pressure, he issued a printed press release that very evening, saying in part:

> From two conversations with Judge Waggoner, we learn unmistakably that the first insult was given by Stark and that he was the first to draw arms and make an attack. We had before understood Stark was unarmed but such was not the case. He was armed with a bowie knife and made two or three lunges at Harrison before the latter fired…In justice to Mr. Harrison, we will say that the statement above, made by Judge Waggoner, presented quite another complexion to the unfortunate transaction on the 12th inst. We await the result of the investigation instituted today, hoping Mr. Harrison will be acquitted of all blame, and shall in our next, give a report of the same.

While Harrison received a retraction from the editor, Byers never saw fit to print a follow-up of the investigation as he stated he would, which, by the way, exonerated Harrison for a second time.

A few weeks later, a handful of members of the lower-class gambling mob—bummers, as they were called—influenced by strong whiskey, invaded Byers's office with threats of death, upon which Byers was marched at gunpoint to the Criterion Saloon. The alcohol-induced plan of the mob was to try Byers in a saloon court for unjustly accusing their supposed friend, Charley Harrison. However, upon their arrival at the Criterion, the self-appointed vigilantes were met by a surprised Harrison. Taking charge of the grave situation, Harrison told the mob to wait while he had a few words with Byers. Taking the editor inside the saloon, Harrison immediately took Byers through the kitchen and out the back door, leading him back to his newspaper office. It was not long before the vigilantes discovered the ruse. The group followed the fleeing pair with leveled guns but withheld their fire for fear of hitting Harrison.

Reaching Byers's office, Harrison advised Byers and his employees to arm themselves. Byers never forgot this act or the fact that Charley Harrison had saved his life, an act that enhanced Harrison's stature in Denver. Yet Byers would continue to be critical of Harrison in his paper if he felt the situation was warranted.

In the fall of 1860, Byers was challenged to a duel by a ferryman on the South Platte River. Undaunted, Byers editorialized: "To anyone who may feel like calling us out, we have only to remark that you are wasting your time. You may murder us, but never on the so-called field of honor."

The duel never commenced, but from then on, Byers wore a gun belt, which carried two Colt revolvers, and became known as the "Fighting Editor."

While he worked hard at staying ahead of the competition, Byers managed to find the time to file a land claim about three miles from Denver City. Here he built a larger framed house for his growing family. In October 1860, fire engulfed the new home. A frantic Elizabeth managed to escape the roaring fire with her three children, snatching her infant son out of his burning crib. Byers was not home during the tragedy. Sadly, the baby died four months later.

The Byers family then moved into a small ranch house on the east side of the South Platte River. It was from this home that Elizabeth turned her personal loss into good for others suffering from misfortune. By mid-winter of 1860, Elizabeth organized the Ladies Union Aid Society. It was the first charitable organization in Denver's history created by the women of the city. The women met in the small home of Mrs. William N. Byers. As president,

Elizabeth guided the group, which provided aid to those in need, struggling in the new, still growing city.

With the fierce newspaper competition, Byers was not only on the cutting edge of the latest technology, but he also became personally involved. When Edward Creighton arrived in Denver, he specifically asked for Byers's help. The *Rocky Mountain News* of September 27, 1866, covered the event, writing, "E. Creighton, of Omaha, general superintendent of western telegraph lines, was in Denver yesterday. To-day [*sic*] he goes to Fort Collins to meet General Dodge, and look along the lines. The new telegraphic line is completed to Laporte."

Byers enthusiastically lent his aid to Edward Creighton's implementation of the telegraph. Byers became an active participant in organizing the United States and Mexico Telegraph Company. During the survey and construction process, Byers walked the entire distance, along with members of his survey crew, from Denver to Santa Fe, New Mexico, in an effort to determine the best route. Through his efforts, telegraph poles were erected along portions of the famed Santa Fe Trail, with a separate route veering north to Denver. It was a long process, yet the telegraph line finally reached Denver in 1868.

In mid-May 1864, an abnormal amount of rain fell along the Platte Valley, swelling the South Platte River and Cherry Creek. At midnight on the night of May 19, the torrential rainfall could no longer be held within the banks of either the river or the creek. Denver City was flooded by a rushing wave of water that took everything in its path. The *Rocky Mountain News* building, constructed in the bed of Cherry Creek, was one of the many businesses washed down the river. O.J. Goldrick, another '59er and a teacher who was also an employee of the *Rocky Mountain News*, wrote a harrowing account of the disaster in its sister paper, the *Commonwealth*, published on May 25, 1864. He recounted, "Higher, broader, deeper, and swifter boiled the waves of water, as the mass of flood, freighted with treasure, trees, and live stock, leaped towards the Blake street bridge, prancing with the violence of a fiery steed stark mad: 'Fierce as ten furies, terrible as hell.'"

Among the many caught in raging floodwaters were members of the Byers family. William, Elizabeth and the children were at their home near the South Platte River that terrible night. As the water rushed over the banks of the river, the couple grabbed their children and climbed onto the roof. Troops from Camp Weld, under the direction of Colonel John Milton Chivington, were able to rescue the family. With the home nearly destroyed, the Byers family stayed at the home of Territorial Governor John Evans and his wife, Margaret Gray Evans.

Following the devastation, destruction and death (nearly two dozen people died), Byers was able to resume publication of the *Rocky Mountain News*, working from the newspaper office of the *Commonwealth*. Within a month, Byers opened new offices for his paper on Larimer Street in the Murdock building, which also housed a billiard room run by another '59er, Count Henri Murat.

The year 1864 turned out to be a tumultuous time for the country, torn apart by the Civil War, as well as for the Territory of Colorado and the Byers family. However, before the year was over, President Abraham Lincoln appointed W.N. Byers postmaster of Denver, a position he held until he resigned in 1867. Elizabeth Byers would later say of this time, "It was the constant anxiety of not knowing what would happen next, rather than any terrible things that actually did happen that made life on the frontier so hard."

In the fall of 1866, Byers opened new offices for the paper in a building he had built at the corner of Larimer and G Streets (today's Sixteenth Street). With several daily papers in circulation, competition for the *Rocky Mountain News* was stiff. Despite the odds, Byers's paper remained the leading newspaper in the growing city of Denver.

The Byers family built their next home at East Colfax and Sherman Streets, in what would become the area known as Capitol Hill. It was from this home that Elizabeth continued her charitable work. She would go on to serve with several charity commissions and was instrumental in forming the Pioneer Ladies Aid Society and its auxiliary, the Society of Colorado Pioneers. Elizabeth also taught a Sunday school class for young adults at the Lawrence Street Methodist Church. In 1872, she established a charity for young women. That same year, Elizabeth, along with her friend Margaret Patten Gray Evans, established the Denver Orphans' Home. With strong encouragement, Mrs. Evans's son, William Gray Evans, president of the Denver Electric and Cable Railway Company, provided free excursion trips for the children.

William Byers had aspirations for running for public office, perhaps even governor, and received encouragement from many of his politician friends. After all, he was the primary promoter of the state, through his newspaper, and, along with the governor, John Evans, brought the first railroad to Denver, the Denver Pacific Railway, on June 17, 1870. Byers's political future looked bright indeed. That lofty goal was soon crushed by scandal.

During the early planning stages of the Denver Pacific Railway, Byers created the Denver Board of Trade, an organization created to secure financial backing for the railroad enterprise. To entice investors, Byers advertised in his newspaper. He received letters of inquiry from all over the country.

One of those many letter writers was Mrs. Hattie E. Sancomb, a divorcée from Lawrence, Kansas. Encouraged by the opportunities expressed by Byers, she arrived in Denver in 1871. After a meeting with Byers, in which she thanked him for his advice and encouragement, she moved to Golden City, where she established a milliner shop. The lovely Hattie Sancomb began writing a series of suggestive notes to Byers. After a brief exchange of letters between the two, the relationship grew intimate. The affair continued for three years.

In 1875, politicians were working toward statehood. If Byers had any chance at gaining the nomination as the first state governor, he had no choice but to end the affair with Hattie Sancomb. This he did. However, a young, scorned Hattie Sancomb did not take rejection well. For several months, she sent threatening letters to Byers and asked him to reconsider. Byers never responded. In January 1876, Sancomb took a bold step. She paid a visit to Mrs. Elizabeth Byers and informed the shocked wife of W.N. Byers of the torrid three-year affair she had with her husband. Later, on March 31, 1876, Sancomb entered the offices of the *Rocky Mountain News*, demanding to see Byers. When employees refused her request, she brandished a pearl-handled revolver. Security quickly diffused the situation. It would be an action she would soon repeat.

On April 5, 1876, after another unsuccessful attempt to meet with Byers at his office, Sancomb happened onto the same horse-drawn trolley Byers was using to make his way home. As the trolley stopped near the Byers's home, Byers embarked from the trolley, as did Sancomb. A heated confrontation ensued, and Sancomb pulled out her revolver. She fired at Byers but missed. Byers managed to grab her and pin her arms behind her back. Elizabeth Byers, hearing the gunshot, peered out the window. Seeing her husband in a distressing situation, she bolted from the house. Driving her buggy at lightning speed, she arrived at the scene. Byers released his attacker and jumped into the buggy. The police were alerted, and it wasn't long before Officer Sanders was able to apprehend Hattie Sancomb.

If ever there was a perfect crime to try in the press, this was it. The owner of the leading newspaper in the city was involved in an affair. The dutiful wife, so beloved by the citizens for her charity work, was viewed by the public as the real victim. The local press had a field day. The *Rocky Mountain News'* most ardent rival competitor, the *Golden Transcript*, was the first to break the story in its April 15 issue. The editor, George West, was not only a friend of

Hattie Sancomb, but he was also a former employee of Byers. It must have given West some sense of pleasure to smear his former newspaper boss in his newspaper with a few of the more scandalous letters Byers had written to Sancomb.

Byers must have been aghast at seeing his "love letters" in print for all to see. Yet it was about to get worse. Reporters from the *Golden Globe* notified Byers that they, too, had copies of his letters to Sancomb—but for $500 in cash, they would not publish them. Byers reflected on the future of his career, his family, his name and his honor. In the end, he paid the *Golden Globe*. Then Byers got serious with his own reporting of the facts of the story that was gripping the city.

The following day, the *Rocky Mountain News* devoted two pages of the April 16 issue to the character of the former Mrs. Hattie Sancomb. The paper prefaced the content with the following statement: "On reviewing the ground, the incidents and her many letters, it becomes very evident that Mrs. H.E. Sancomb became satisfied, about a year ago, that her game was safely trapped, and that she might proceed with her 'bear-baiting' in her own way, and at her own time, doubtless expecting the offer of a large amount of 'hush money.'"

Following that statement, a series of letters written by Sancomb to Byers were printed. Dated June 3, 1875, Sancomb wrote, "I have dedicated the rest of my life to your misery. You are only dear to me as an object of revenge. Send me a letter, I say, or I will one day pierce her heart with a dozen bullets. Oh infernal villain, if I had you here I'd plant my fingers in your eyes and tear them from their sockets."

Exactly a month later, on July 3, 1875, the vindictive vixen wrote, "You can do nothing now to save you or your family. Ah, my friend, such letters as the one this morning will not do for me. A letter with kisses quiets me in measure. Without them all is lost but my thirst for revenge."

And then, on January 15, 1876, nearly three months prior to the attempted shooting of Byers, Sancomb prophetically wrote, "I will take you on the street—anywhere. All I ask is a glimpse of you, and my bullet will be aimed."

For his part in the affair, Byers readily admitted his culpability but also revealed the accounts of blackmail and threats to his family, particularly his wife. His editorial went on to state that it had "become necessary" to come forward in the press to correct the record regarding the "distorted and false" statements presented in the *Golden Transcript*. He went on to report that Mrs. Hattie Sancomb's husband had previously secured a divorce on the grounds of adultery with one Colonel Burns. O.J. Goldrick, Byers's old friend, editorialized from his latest paper, the *Denver Herald*, in such a way as only Goldrick could that "the sensational versions of the affair only show the animus of the exposé against the editor and owner of the *News*, as an available piece of property for plucking, on the plea of 'injured innocence,' chaste-ned [*sic*] 'heart-aches,' virgin virtues, tender throbbing, Kansas blue-grass, spring chickens, and 'sich.'"

Two weeks later, the preliminary trial was held in a Denver courtroom. Of the many newspaper reporters who covered the event, one wrote of the accused, Hattie Sancomb, "She sat demurely in the harsh glare of the courtroom with eyes of coal gray tint, regular features, dazzling teeth, penciled eyebrows, small poised head and wavy auburn hair. Her voice was soft and her manner caressing."

In a final twist to the sordid affair, played out in the pages of the Denver newspapers, the judge left the case on the docket. It never came to trial. Yet, Byers was damaged politically. In June of that same year, the political parties held their caucuses and eventually nominated their candidates for the upcoming election. William N. Byers, a true pioneer and one of the founders of the Republican Party in the Colorado territory, was not even mentioned as a candidate for any office.

On May 4, 1878, William Newton Byers stepped down from the board of his *Rocky Mountain News* enterprise, ostensibly to focus on his many business endeavors. His final editorial appeared in the May 16, 1878 issue of the paper, where he wrote in part:

> *With this issue my pecuniary interest in and editorial control of the* Rocky Mountain News *ceases. The News Printing Company continues with but a single change in its directory, and will conduct the publication of the* News, *as well as all the varied branches of the business that have grown up with and around it. This assurance, however, I can give: that it is backed by plenty of capital to keep it at the front. Friends who have feared its failure may dismiss their alarm. Enemies who have hoped for its downfall may possess their souls in peace. Toward my brethren of the press I have none but the kindest feelings. All differences are forgotten and only pleasant recollections of them shall dwell in my memory.*

The same year that Byers relinquished control of his pioneer newspaper, he served a second term as postmaster of Denver from 1879 to 1883. He also continued his business relationship with his friend John Evans and his son, William Gray Evans, and their Denver Electric and Cable Railway

Company, a company they had started together some years previously. Byers was also involved with the Denver, Texas & Fort Worth Railroad, which would eventually reach Denver in 1888.

During this troubling time, Elizabeth Byers remained with her husband, continuing her work with philanthropic groups.

Glory Days

William Newton Byers purchased land in the heart of the residential area on the eastern edge of the commerce district of downtown Denver. It was here that in 1883, Byers built a modest mansion for he and Elizabeth, as both Mary and Frank had married and begun their own lives.

Located at Thirteenth and Bannock Streets, the two-story, wine-colored brick residence, built in the popular Italianate style of the time, was enhanced with decorative cornices. Wrought-iron fencing protected the tiny lawn facing Bannock Street.

Inside, guests were greeted in the formal parlor. This room included an ornate, silver-plated clock, as well as a grand fireplace, graced with two intricately decorated urns at each end. The ceiling was beautifully hand painted. The focal point of the large front room was the beautiful bay window. The dining room, with leaded-glass windows, provided wonderful lighting to the room, which featured a long table and decorative wallpaper. The spacious kitchen included a state-of-the-art stove and an enormous wooden icebox, capable of holding fifty pounds of ice, which was delivered daily.

An ornate stairway led to the bedrooms and bathrooms, as well as servants' quarters on the second floor. This floor consisted of the master bedroom and several guest rooms. One of the guest bathrooms featured a porcelain tub, elevated with an ornate Victorian brass claw design.

While William and Elizabeth Byers lived in this home, they both continued their various business and charitable interests. Social gatherings and meetings in their home led to the forming of the forerunner of the Denver Chamber of Commerce, the Society of Colorado Pioneers, and the formation of the State Historical and Natural History Society.

William Byers continued to be a force in Denver's growing economic future. In 1886, he, along with John Evans and his son, William Gray Evans, incorporated their Denver Electric and Cable Railway Company into the newly formed Denver Tramway Company. John Evans served as president,

Byers as vice-president and W.G. Evans as secretary. The Denver Tramway Company, under the leadership of Byers and the father-and-son Evans duo, secured an exclusive city franchise under mayor Joseph E. Bates to build electric streetcar lines throughout the downtown area of Denver.

Meanwhile, Elizabeth was involved with the creation of the Women's Club of Denver, a group of married and single women who had careers apart from their duties at home. Elizabeth served as president of the large group, which included many women, such as Margaret Evans, who would go on to be leaders in the suffragist movement. In 1894, Elizabeth was also instrumental in the founding of the Denver Woman's Club, an umbrella organization of sorts that encompassed all women organizations. Sara Decker Platt served as the first president of this group. Dues were five dollars a year. Elizabeth Byers later said, "I always considered I raised Denver. Yes, indeed, we pioneer women raised her from a lusty, noisy infant to the sedate, beautiful city she is today."

William and Elizabeth Byers lived in the Bannock Street home for six years, eventually selling the residence in 1889.

And the Rest Is History

William and Elizabeth Byers sold their home to William Gray Evans, Byers's longtime business partner and the son of his good friend and partner, former territorial governor John Evans. Byers and the former governor had worked together on several ventures during the early days of Denver, including the monumental effort to bring the railroads to Denver and the founding of the Colorado Seminary, later the University of Denver.

William and Cornelia Lunt Evans moved into the former Byers home with their two young children, John and Josephine. A third child, Margaret, named for her grandmother, was born in the home that December, as was their fourth child, Katherine, born in 1894. For nearly a century, various Evans family members would occupy the mansion home.

William and Cornelia Evans would make several changes to the mansion over the years. In 1898, a two-story addition was added to the south side. This allowed for a library, as well as additional bedrooms and bathrooms. William Evans so enjoyed his library that he once described the room as "the nicest place on earth."

An important Denver business and civic leader, Evans remained at the helm of the Denver Tramway Company while also serving as a board

William Gray Evans, son of former territorial governor John Evans, bought the home from William Byers in 1889. *Denver Public Library.*

member for several banking and railroad institutions. William Evans joined in a partnership with Colorado's railroad tycoon, David Moffat, in building the Moffat Tunnel through a portion of the Continental Divide. Evans was instrumental in gaining the financing for the monumental project through his banking connections in New York.

Members of the Evans family relax on the porch and lawn of their new home. *Denver Public Library.*

Unfortunately, David Moffat died before his namesake tunnel was completed. William Evans was with Moffat at the time of his death in April 1911. Following the death of David Moffat, Evans took over Moffat's position as president of the Denver, Northwestern & Pacific Railway, as well as becoming president of Moffat's Colorado-Utah Construction Company.

Assuming the duties of Moffat's former offices provided Evans the opportunity to continue the work the two men had started in building the Moffat Tunnel. After several years of legal negotiations and engineering difficulties in building such a monumental tunnel, the project was finally completed on February 18, 1927. Blasting through the Continental Divide, the 6.2-mile tunnel provided a link between Denver and Colorado's western slope. The Denver & Salt Lake Railroad was the first to run its line through the tunnel in the spring of 1927.

Following the death of John Evans on July 3, 1897, William G. Evans assumed his father's duties as president of the Denver Tramway Company (DTC). By 1900, under W.G. Evans's leadership, the DTC had driven its competition, the cable car and horse railways, out of business and monopolized streetcar service in the Denver metro area. It was modern ingenuity and the wave of the future. The DTC then installed a citywide network of electric trolleys, powered by overhead electric lines that reached nearly every neighborhood in Denver.

Shortly after the death of his father, William, for unknown reasons, transferred the deed of the Bannock Street home over to his wife, Cornelia Evans. It was also at this time that Cornelia's widowed father, Captain William Patten Gray, moved into the home. Later, William invited his mother, Margaret, and his unmarried sister, Anne, to also move into his Bannock Street home. It is interesting to note that Cornelia's father and William's mother were brother and sister, making Cornelia and William first cousins.

In 1900, another addition to the home was built to accommodate the new occupants. This new two-story addition created a separate apartment occupied by Margaret and her daughter, Anne. The arrangement included a parlor room with two fireplaces and an elevator that rose to the second floor. The upper floor consisted of a master bedroom decorated in bright yellow, highlighted with a carved wooden bed. A large sitting room, again decorated in yellow, was filled with many of Anne's paintings.

When Mayor Robert Walker Speer launched his "City Beautiful" project shortly after his election in 1904, he used the Evanses' original 1894 park proposal and asked William G. Evans to participate in the implementation. Evans enthusiastically agreed. The project began in 1909, and over the next four years, a fabulous park network was constructed throughout the city. William G. Evans saw the project through to its completion, which would have pleased his father. In 1913, he retired from the Denver Tramway Company, spending many of his golden years in his beloved library in his Bannock Street home.

Following the deaths of William and Cornelia Evans, Anne remained in the home. Her sisters, Josephine and Katherine, neither of whom had ever married, eventually moved into the Evans home with Anne. Margaret Evans Davis, the youngest of Anne's sisters, moved back into the family home following her husband's death and would be the last Evans family member to occupy the home.

At the age of sixty-nine, Anne Evans died in her family home in 1941. Josephine died in the house in 1969, at the age of eighty-two. Katherine also died in the home in 1977 at the age of eighty-three. Margaret, the youngest child of the former territorial governor, remained in the Evans home. In 1978, following the death of William Gray Evans's son, John, his heirs, along with Margaret's family, agreed to donate the historic home as well as the contents, to the Colorado Historical Society, with the stipulation that Margaret Evans Davis be allowed to live in the home until her death.

Margaret Evans Davis died in the home in 1981, at the age of ninety-two. She was both the first of the Evans family to be born in the home and the last of the family to live in the residence.

Today

Following the death of Margaret Evans Davis, the Colorado Historical Society took possession of the mansion, along with its entire contents. Restoration of the residence began with the intent of opening it to the public as a museum.

During renovation, the formal parlor's original hand-painted ceiling was discovered. It had been heavily discolored from the early use of gas lighting. The original design was copied onto canvas and placed just below the original ceiling.

It took years to restore the historic mansion to its current 1912–24 appearance. When it was completed in 1990, the Colorado Historical Society opened it to the public as the Byers-Evans House Museum.

Visitors are treated to a tour of the mansion, which served as the home of two of Colorado's prominent pioneers. Because of the Evans family's longevity in the home—ninety-two years—most of the history and family heirlooms focus on that particular family. However, one of the formal parlors, for there are two, contains the only items in the home that once belonged to the Byers family. An ornate, silver-plated clock and two urns are exhibited on the fireplace mantle.

The focal points of the large front room are the gramophone and the grand piano often played by Margaret. In the dining room, the elegant table is set with the eight-piece set of Haviland china purchased by Governor Evans's wife, Margaret, in 1888. Each piece is engraved with gold lettering on the backside. The cozy library remains much as it did when William Gray Evans called it "the nicest place on earth."

The spacious kitchen, brightened by a high skylight added during the time period depicted, is a highlight on the tour. While the house was later updated with modern appliances, the Evans family had saved the original stove and tall wooden icebox from the time the Byerses lived in the home. It is prominently displayed in the kitchen area.

The 1900 addition features Anne Evans's bright-yellow sitting room and displays several of Anne's paintings, as well as many handmade pottery pieces.

A bit out of place today, the modest two-story brick 1883 Byers-Evans mansion at 1310 Bannock Street shares the street block with the massive Denver Art Museum. When it was built, the home was in the heart of the residential area on the southwest edge of the original commerce district of downtown Denver. Today, it is the oldest mansion in the oldest residential area originally platted for Denver City.

Fun Facts

- When Byers arrived in Denver City with his two wagons of printing supplies and the printing press on the evening of April 20, 1859, one of the wagons became stuck in the soft, sandy bed of Cherry Creek. It was nearly dawn before the wagon was pulled through wet sloppy sand.
- It is said that in the spring of 1859, when Elizabeth Byers arrived in Denver City and saw her crudely built cabin, she wept.
- Charley Harrison left Denver City to join the Confederacy when the Civil War broke out. He always considered W.N. Byers a friend and later sent him a gold ring. Although Byers kept the ring, he never wore it.
- During the disastrous flood of 1864, the city safe, containing court and probate records, was washed downstream. It was never found.
- The Ladies Union Aid Society, founded by Mrs. Elizabeth Byers, made nightshirts, underwear and bandages for Colorado's military Volunteer Regiment.
- The Byers-Evans House was placed on the National Register on August 25, 1970, 5DV.163.

Contact Information

BYERS-EVANS HOUSE MUSEUM
1310 Bannock Street
Denver, Colorado 80204
www.historycolorado.org
(303) 620-4933

Chapter 3

THE ROBISON MANSION—CANON CITY—1884

THE PRIDE OF A CITY'S HISTORY

"The handsome and modern residence erected by Lyman Robison in South Canon, is one of the most lovely building sites in this part of the country."

The Beginning

As reported in the *Canon City Record* newspaper of August 1, 1885, the Robison mansion did indeed become one of Canon City's finest residences.

Lyman Robison was born October 23, 1837, in Wooster, Ohio. He grew up on the family farm, and following his education, he entered the mercantile business. With the outbreak of the Civil War, he joined the Union army in 1861. Following an illness that took him out of military service, he reenlisted in 1864 with the Forty-fourth Infantry of Iowa, serving until the end of the war in 1865. Robison returned to his native state of Ohio, where he resumed his employment in the mercantile business. Here, he married the former Mary Roadnight, and their only surviving child, David Lyman, was born on October 23, 1877, in Toledo, Ohio.

With news of a second rich ore strike in Colorado Territory—this time silver—Robison, along with thousands, heeded the call for the West, bound for riches. Very few found wealth, but Robison did. Arriving in Leadville, Colorado, in 1878, Robison invested in several mining properties. The incredible riches of Leadville's silver mines made Robison a wealthy man.

Although it was Leadville's mines that made Robison's fortune, the high altitude and harsh winters did not agree with his wife, Mary. Seeking relief from the severe cold, the Robisons spent the winter seasons in Canon City. By 1884, the Robisons had made Canon City their permanent home.

Glory Days

In 1884, Robison hired the architectural firm of Marean and Norton to design his mansion on four acres located near the Arkansas River. The land, five hundred by three hundred feet and offering a commanding view of the river, was a perfect spot for Canon City's finest residence. The Robison home would be built facing the river.

The three-story brick edifice, built in the Second Empire style, was constructed of native sandstone and pressed bricks from the local Catlin brickyard. The exterior of the Robison home included two-story bay windows on both the east and west sides of the mansion. The mansard roof, covered with metal shingles, was surrounded by a wide heavy cornice and included a cast-iron widow's walk. Gothic windows graced the upper portion of the mansion.

A two-story porch at the entrance was supported by classic marble columns. A second porch and patio, at the rear, allowed for outdoor entertainment. The grounds were well landscaped, including trees, shrubs and flowers, and were surrounded by an iron fence set on a sandstone foundation.

A large two-story brick barn located behind the mansion completed the Robison property. The building was designed and built by well-known local architect George W. Roe, hired by Robison to supervise the construction of the barn. The structure was capped by a mansard roof measuring an incredible forty-five by forty-seven feet. The ground floor contained stalls for horses, two cow stalls and an area for two buggies. An elevated rack for washing wagons was also installed. The second story contained a large hayloft, a harness room and sleeping quarters for the stable help. The building was completed with a large octagonal ventilator, which allowed a continuous flow of fresh air to pass through the building.

The interior of the Robison mansion, over six thousand square feet, was nothing short of a construction wonder. The brick walls were sixteen inches thick on the first floor and twelve inches thick on the second and third floors. Local brick worker Frans Sell is credited with the magnificent brick and stone work throughout the mansion. Extreme detail went into several aspects of the home. Robison hired highly qualified local carpenter C.J. Smith, who added his special touch to the doors and windows. The caps of all the windows and doors were detailed with Berlin stone and elegantly chiseled in the latest stonecutter style. The Robisons' new home reflected a quality of design and richness of detail unmatched in Canon City.

On the main floor, the formal parlor room and the second parlor room both included five- by eleven-foot bay windows, lending an air of opulence. The ceilings were enhanced with a rose-and-leaf motif painted in gold. The sitting room and dining room were graced with sixteen-foot ceilings, many of which were detailed with fresco artwork. From the ceilings, fine chandeliers enhanced the rooms with their light. The Honduran mahogany winding staircase, imported from Austria and entirely handcrafted using no nails, rose in grand splendor through the three stories of the mansion. The three fireplaces in the home were imported from Italy, and their ornamental tiling and mahogany woodwork complemented the grand stairway.

The kitchen, a technological wonder, extended to the second floor. The first floor of the kitchen, with its eleven-foot ceiling, included the finest of appliances available, as well as a large pantry and a china closet. The second floor of the kitchen, a scaled-down version of the main kitchen, catered to the private needs of the family.

The second floor contained the family bedrooms, rooms for the servants and a bathroom. The third floor had two large rooms with hardwood flooring, intended for social parties, dancing and family entertainment. When the mansion was completed two years later, it became the social center for the elite in Canon City. The citizens were thrilled with the new residence, as it represented class and refinement in their town. The *Canon City Record* declared, "This magnificent structure which, while being a great credit to Canon, is a lasting monument of Mr. Robison's appreciation of the city of his adoption and mark of his confidence in its future…that Mr. Robison came here to make this place his permanent home and not simply for his health the *Record* is glad to chronicle the completion of his residence, the handsomest in Southern Colorado."

Due to Robison's wealth and influence, his social events at the mansion hosted many of the state's wealthy businessmen and politicians, including the governor and senators. Robison's wife, Mary, was also interested in the social growth of the city and hosted many fundraisers in her home. Their annual New Year's Eve party was the social event of the season in Canon City. It was a lavish affair, including a formal dinner, followed by dancing with music provided by a full-piece orchestra. Then, at midnight, the guests

Lyman Robison built his Canon City mansion in 1884. *Courtesy Royal Gorge History Center.*

would welcome in the New Year complete with champagne and party favors. James Peabody, a successful Canon City merchant and former mayor of the town, was a good friend of Robison. Peabody and his wife attended the annual celebration for many years, and Peabody was a distinguished guest during his term as governor of the state from 1903 to 1905.

And the Rest Is History

Robison became instrumental in the economy and growth of Canon City. He built and promoted three of the town's biggest business blocks, the Apex, Annex and Sulphide blocks, named after his mining investments, which became the core business district of Canon City.

Meanwhile, Robison remained active with his mining interests. In 1892, he and business partner J.J. Cone were successful in the development of the Doctor

Mine in the Cripple Creek Mining District. With the rich ore production of his latest mining venture, Robison again gave back to the town of Canon City.

In 1899, Robison was one of the founders of the Portland Cement Company. He served as vice-president and director of the First National Bank of Canon City. He also served for a time as the president of the Royal Gorge Hot Springs and Company. He later purchased a lot at Harrison Avenue and Eighth Street, only to donate it to the Christ Episcopal Church. Lyman and Mary Robison were also among the largest contributors to the church building fund. In 1900, he headed the South Canon Ditch Company, which is still in use to this day.

David Lyman Robison married Maud Morey in 1902. As a wedding gift, his parents presented him with a new house near the family mansion. David, who made his living in the insurance business, lived in the home with Maud and their two children: Margaret, born 1904, and Lyman, born 1907.

In 1901, Lyman and Mary Robison made improvements to the mansion, including a classical portico with Tuscan columns at the entrance to the home. Continuing their social events held at the mansion, the Robisons' activities were often covered in the local papers. One such event was reported in the *Canon City Daily Record*, dated November 1905:

> *A delightful reception and dance were given at Annex Hall by Mr. and Mrs. Lyman Robison and Mr. and Mrs. David Robison to commemorate the 39th wedding anniversary of the former. It has been the custom for them to give a reception to their friends on each recurring anniversary of their marriage and these events have long been regarded as among the most pleasing in the social chronicles of the city as they are excellent entertainers.*

Sadly, just six months later, sixty-year-old Mary Robison died on May 16, 1906. The death of his wife struck Lyman Robison particularly hard, and his health began to decline. He stayed active in his various business interests as long as possible. On January 8, 1912, at the age of seventy-four, Lyman Robison died.

After the death of his father, David and his family moved into the mansion. David was involved in many local activities including the Chamber of Commerce Highway committee, the Canon City Museum Board, the Red Cross Board of Directors and the Fremont County Draft Board during World War II. He and Maud were influential in many community celebrations, including Fruit Day and the Fremont County Fair.

When Maud died in 1929, David was devastated. The economic disaster following the stock market crash that same year only fueled David's despair.

The servants were let go one by one.

For the next twenty-nine years, David lived alone in the family home. During the Great Depression of the 1930s, the mansion fell into a state of serious disrepair, whether due to the depressed economy or David's lonely life. Nevertheless, Canon City's prized residence became an eyesore.

In 1958, David Lyman Robison, now in poor health, sold the family home. It was bought by the publisher of the *Canon City Daily Record* newspaper, Donald Hardy. His idea was to refurbish the mansion and open it to the public in the form of a museum. Lacking the needed funds, he offered it the city for $17,000. When the Canon City officials declined the offer, Hardy put the historic property on the market. He sold it in 1961 for $21,000 to Mr. and Mrs. Roy Wilson who, in turn, announced their intentions to tear down the historic mansion. The *Pueblo Chieftain Star Journal* reported the story in its February 10, 1963 issue with a bold headline "Canon City Landmark to be Destroyed."

The article went on to state that the Wilsons intended to turn the property into a rest home. The citizens of Canon City were outraged that the historic property would be torn down. Due to the public outcry, the Wilsons reconsidered. After considerable restoration, they opened the mansion to the public as a museum. The Wilsons operated the museum for several years. By 1976, Edith, now a widow, could no longer handle the enormous upkeep and expense required to maintain the mansion museum. Mrs. Wilson was forced to sell the historic edifice at auction.

The Robison mansion was purchased by Kenneth and Naomi Ireland, who moved into the home with their young family in 1979. They were the first to call the mansion home in over two decades. The Irelands made further improvements in the mansion, keeping to the historical integrity of the original owners. In 1984, through their restoration efforts and research, they were able to get the property placed on the National Register of Historic Places.

However, it was during the Irelands' ownership that the Robison historic barn was sold to Janie Workman of Canon City. She converted the barn into a carriage house, where she operated Janie's Chile Wagon for a number of years.

Following Naomi Ireland's death, Kenneth eventually listed the Robison property for sale. The asking price was $300,000. A local Canon City citizen, Edward Tezak, bought the historic property in 1989 for $200,000.

Tezak had extensive work done to both the exterior and interior of the mansion, as well as the grounds. Particular attention was given to the interior of the ninety-year-old historic structure, returning it to its former glory. Modern conveniences were installed as well, including central air conditioning and updating the plumbing and electricity. Tezak installed the Victorian-era push-button light switches and brass vent coverings for the heating system. He also purchased Victorian wallpaper and carpet, ornate wallcoverings, draperies and furniture, which were installed throughout the mansion. Five-foot chandeliers, imported from Italy, graced the rooms with their light. The ceiling in the formal dining room was painted in gold, enhanced with Victorian filigree.

The exterior received the same attention to detail, including upgrading all of the ironwork. The foundation of the mansion was restored to its original appearance, and the brown paint that had covered the exterior sandstone blocks was removed. The damaged blocks were replaced with matching sandstone blocks from a historic hotel in Alamosa, since closed. The basement of the mansion received extensive work. Tezak's contractors lowered the floor by eighteen inches and installed a sandstone floor, using the matching sandstone from the Alamosa hotel. The enlarged basement included a large wine cellar, capable of holding over two thousand bottles of fine wine, complete with a locking iron gate for added protection. A separate room was added, resembling an old English pub.

Additionally, the exterior wood trim was repaired and repainted in a complementary color common to the Victorian era. A large, round, European-style fountain graced the manicured lawns, and a semicircular brick driveway completed the work.

After spending over $1 million in restoration, Tezak next turned his attention to the former barn, now known fondly as the "Carriage House." He purchased the building, with the intention of using it as public hall for special occasions and weddings. Unfortunately, he ran into zoning and licensing issues with the city officials. Unable to resolve the problems, Tezak eventually sold the property in 1998 to Joe and Kathleen Wells for $650,000. The Wells applied for and were able to obtain a historic grant for repairs to the roof. The overall upkeep of the mansion eventually forced the Wellses to attempt to sell at auction in 2000. However, the property did not sell.

Darryl Biggerstaff, a real estate investor, bought the Robison mansion and grounds for over $1 million in 2004. Biggerstaff had a storied life. Born in Arizona on April 27, 1939, he left home at the age of fourteen to live with his sisters in Nebraska. He eventually attended college in that state. Following college, he worked in the banking industry. Relocating to Canon City, he served as chairman of the board for the Fremont National Bank and the Canon National Bank. In Canon City, he soon began investing in real estate. Biggerstaff became a very wealthy man, and he was a generous benefactor to the community. In order to save the James Peabody mansion from demolition, he also purchased that historic property and then sold it at an affordable price to the city as part of the downtown revitalization and urban renewal effort. Biggerstaff also contributed to the city's Fremont Campus of Pueblo Community College. For his philanthropy, he was given the Distinguished Citizens Award by the Canon City Chamber of Commerce. In 2006, Biggerstaff's name was added to the "Outstanding Civic Leaders of Canon City" plaque. The inscription reads: "Darryl Biggerstaff, Banker-Philanthropist, 1990 Distinguished Citizen, Community Leader and Fundraiser, Pueblo Community College Fremont Campus, 2006."

Unfortunately, Biggerstaff died not long after he purchased the Robison mansion. The historic property passed to his heir, Heather Biggerstaff-Cost. Once again, the Robison mansion was put on the auction block. Again, the mansion did not sell. It eventually went on the market with an asking price of $1,495,500. The *Canon City Daily Record* ran the headline: "Victorian-Style Historic Landmark Mansion and Home for Sale Again in Colorado"

Today

Robison's 1884 three-story brick mansion with its mansard roof is one of the very few well-preserved examples of the Second Empire style of architecture remaining in Colorado. The residence also illustrates a unique quality of design and detail unmatched in the Canon City area.

In 2008, the entire four acres of the historic Robison property was transferred to HLC Enterprises LLC, which is managed by Erin Tierney, along with her son and his wife, Mr. and Mrs. James Characky Jr. The family's goal is to maintain the integrity of the Historic Robison Mansion and Carriage House as Darryl Biggerstaff intended.

After a few renovations, the Robison mansion was ready to once again receive visitors. In 2011, the company opened the property to the public for the first time in thirty-five years.

Today, the Robison mansion and property is host to a variety of events, including corporate business retreats, vacation rentals, special occasions, reunions and weddings. Outdoor features for such events include a gazebo with electricity; the courtyard; the three-thousand-square-foot carriage house, with both an indoor and outdoor dance floor; and an outdoor sound system.

Inside, the Robison Mansion offers rooms for vacation rentals, reunions and weddings. The guests are treated to the opulence of the Victorian atmosphere,

The dining room is decorated in rich Victorian décor. *Andrea Mauriello.*

The master suite of the Robison mansion. *Andrea Mauriello.*

Contemporary exterior of the Robison Mansion. *Beel Photography.*

decorated with antique furnishings typical of the era. The fully equipped kitchen, remodeled and updated with Viking appliances, while retaining nothing of the original kitchen, is capable of providing for the largest social events. The mansion's three travertine bathrooms include dual Rain Shower heads.

In addition, the Robison mansion hosts an annual Christmas tour, open to the general public, a fundraising event in conjunction with local nonprofit organizations. It is an event Lyman and Mary Robison would be quite pleased with.

Fun Facts

- The barn erected on the Robison property was "the largest, most complete barn in the county," according to the *Canon City Record* newspaper of August 1, 1885.
- A couple interesting events occurred during the ownership of the mansion during the period of 1961 to 1976. During this period, what few original pieces belonging to the Robisons that were left in the house—such as furniture, paintings and other artifacts—were sold. It was also during this time that a beautifully carved sign was hung in the yard. Unfortunately, the Robison name was spelled "Robinson."
- During one of the many restorations, a section of original wallpaper was uncovered in a hallway. A piece of this Victorian wallpaper is displayed in a glass case on the second floor of the mansion.
- Today, the altar at the Christ Episcopal Church is a memorial to Mrs. Mary Robison given by one of the church guilds.
- The Robison Mansion was placed on the National Register on October 11, 1984, 5FN.99.

Contact Information

ROBISON MANSION & CARRIAGE HOUSE
12 Riverside Drive
Canon City, Colorado 81212
www.robisonmansion.com
(719) 345-4105

Chapter 4

THE MOLLY BROWN HOUSE—DENVER—1887

THE HOUSE OF LIONS

The Beginning

Colorado's rich mining industry not only brought a wealth of income to the area, but it was also an economic force that eventually led to statehood in 1876. The infant mining-supply town of Denver City, situated perfectly near the South Platte River and Cherry Creek confluence, grew to become Colorado's cultured capital.

Several of Colorado's rich mine owners chose Denver as the place to build their homes. Denver's Capitol Hill area was favored by many of these mining tycoons. In 1887, George W. Clayton began the construction of an exquisite home for Isaac N. and Mary Large. For unknown reasons, William A. Lang later replaced Clayton as the architect of the home.

Mr. Large had gained his wealth in Colorado silver mining investments and wanted a splendid home in Denver that reflected his stature. To that end, Lang designed one of Denver's finest—yet modest—mansions.

Located on a small lot on Pennsylvania Avenue (later changed to Street), the three-story home was built in the Queen Anne style, popular in Denver at the time. The exterior was constructed of rough-cut pink stone and gray rhyolite. The terra cotta–trimmed roof was complemented by three A-framed sections, two on the front of the home and the third on the north side. Facing west, the porch, sunroom and upper-floor windows offered

J.J. and Margaret Brown purchased this fashionable Denver mansion in 1894. *Denver Public Library.*

magnificent views of the Rocky Mountains. Sandstone steps led to the open A-framed portico and entrance to the mansion. A two-story sandstone carriage house was built on the back of the lot.

Inside the home, the entrance hall with hardwood floors and matching wood staircase were complemented by Victorian wallpaper. A large parlor room, a library with floor-to-ceiling mahogany bookshelves, an elegant dining room and a kitchen were all located on the first floor. There were four fireplaces, although the home was constructed with forced-air heating. The second and third floors contained several bedrooms and two bathrooms. A second stairway was used by the servants and led to the kitchen.

The mansion was one of the first in Denver to include such modern conveniences as electricity, indoor hot and cold running water and the newest of features, a hand-crank telephone. The many windows that graced the mansion were designed by Denver artist M. Watkins, who also designed the beautiful round stained-glass window featured on the second floor of Lang's Raymond House, later known as Castle Marne.

The Issac Large family moved into the home when it was completed in 1890. The couple often hosted social and business gatherings. A frequent guest was David Hyman, a founder of the town of Aspen and a personal friend and business associate of Large.

Unfortunately, in 1893, when the government repealed the Sherman Silver Purchase Act, which had allowed for silver as a monetary backing to the U.S. dollar, the country fell into a severe economic depression. With the silver-mining industry being one of the state's major economic contributors, Colorado was particularly affected. Several mines across the state closed down nearly overnight, and many who had made their fortunes in silver went broke. Conversely, the price of gold, now the only metal ore backing the country's currency, rose to enormous prices.

Isaac N. Large was one of those men who suffered financially from the silver crash of 1893. As a result, he was forced to sell his home on Pennsylvania Avenue.

Due to the economic depression and the closing of silver mines, many of the mine owners and business owners who had made their wealth in silver and were able to withstand the crash moved to Denver, while the many mine workers and their families were devastated. One of these men who survived the depression was James Joseph (J.J.) Brown. On April 6, 1894, Brown purchased the mansion from the Large family for $30,000 and "a certain trust deed for $12,500."

When the purchase of their home was finalized, Brown; his wife, Margaret; and their two children, seven-year-old Lawrence and five-year-old Catherine Ellen, celebrated the event during a spring snowstorm with a sleigh ride on Pennsylvania Avenue.

Glory Days

James Joseph Brown, the son of Irish immigrants John and Cecilia Palmer Brown, was born in Waymart, Wayne County, Pennsylvania, on September 27, 1854. Following his schooling, he went to work in the Pennsylvania coal mines. In February 1877, at the age of twenty-three, Brown made his way west.

Brown first worked in the gold mines in the Black Hills of Dakota Territory. After two years, with a bit of knowledge and experience, he moved on to work in the silver mining area of Aspen, Colorado. It was here that he met influential mining men who would become lifelong friends. However, on a salary of four dollars a day, Brown, an intelligent and ambitious man, left Aspen for better opportunities. In 1882, he moved to Leadville, known as the "silver capital of the world." Brown found work in the local mines, and at night, he studied geology and mining technology.

His efforts paid off. In 1885, he was hired as a shift manager for a group of silver mines owned by David Moffat and Eben Smith. Deeper exploration was required, digging shafts into the earth and rock. Due to his knowledge, work ethic and dedication, Brown was promoted to foreman and then superintendent of the Louisville, the Maid and the Henriette mines, which were some of the richest mines in Leadville. Over the next fourteen years, Brown improved the mining technology and boosted the profits of his company. He became well known as a competent mining engineer throughout the area. The *Leadville Herald Democrat* declared Brown "one of the best mine superintendents in the district."

It was in Leadville that he met a fiery, blue-eyed, red-haired Irish Catholic lass by the name of Margaret Tobin. The two were both in attendance at a Catholic church picnic in the early summer of 1886. A whirlwind courtship soon began.

Margaret Tobin was born on July 18, 1867, in the Mississippi River town of Hannibal, Missouri, the same town where Samuel Langhorne Clemens grew up and later wrote of his childhood experiences under the pseudonym Mark Twain. Her father, John, and her stepmother, Johanna, had a small home in the area known as Shantytown. John worked at the Hannibal Gas Works, and Johanna managed the household, raised the children, saw to their education and insisted on proper Catholic religious training.

Maggie, as she was fondly called by her family (she was never called Molly in her lifetime), went to work at the local Garth Tobacco Factory at the age of thirteen to help with the family's finances. The hours were long, the work was dirty and it required extensive physical labor. While Maggie worked hard at her job six days a week, she hated it, but the strong work ethic stuck with her for the rest of her life.

Maggie's older half-sister Mary Ann and her husband, Jack Landrigan, left for Leadville in 1883. Three years later, Maggie and her older brother, Daniel, left on a westbound train for Colorado to join their sister. Arriving in Leadville, Maggie lived with her sister and brother-in-law and quickly found employment at the Daniels, Fisher & Smith Emporium on Leadville's main thoroughfare of Harrison Street. Again, her strong work ethic proved to be her greatest asset, and she became a valued employee.

Joseph J.J. Brown. *Denver Public Library.*

The courtship of J.J. Brown and Margaret Tobin began with a mutual interest in the theater, and they often attended performances at the Tabor Opera House in Leadville. Long carriage rides and picnics followed. After a six-month courtship, the couple was married on September 1, 1886. The groom was thirty-one years old, and the bride had just turned nineteen. The wedding ceremony took place in the Catholic Annunciation Church in Leadville, officiated by Leadville's respected pioneer Catholic priest, Father Henry Robinson. Among the many wedding gifts received was a splendid solid silver tea service from the miners of the Leadville mines.

The *Leadville Herald Democrat* reported the wedding nuptials, with obvious approval of the union, in its September 2, 1886 issue:

> *An event that commands a prominent place in the social and hymenial [sic] records of the year was the marriage of Mr. J.J. Brown, the popular superintendent of the Louisville mine to Miss Maggie Tobin, the accomplished young saleslady for whom the patrons of Messrs. Daniels, Fisher & Smith's will invoke the richest blessings. The contracting parties are, in fact, both well-known to the good people with whom they have been cast in the Cloud City, and no two could elicit more sincere expressions of approval than those which have been listened to at this time.*

Following the wedding, the couple lived briefly at 322 West Seventh Street in Leadville. Later they moved closer to the mines where Brown worked, a small mining camp called Stumpftown. Here, the couple lived in a small two-room cabin. It was a rugged existence. Water had to be pumped from the only well in the camp and then hauled back to their cabin. This was their home for the next few years.

Maggie gave birth to their first child, Lawrence Palmer, on August 30, 1887. A daughter, Catherine Ellen, who was called Helen, joined the family on July 1, 1889. With a growing family, the Browns moved back into Leadville, where they bought a modest clapboard house at 300 East Seventh Street. Maggie began extensive tutoring sessions with Mrs. Wooster, where she was instructed in literature, art and music. This was also about the time when Maggie's father and stepmother, John and Johanna, sold their home in Hannibal and moved to Leadville, bringing with them Maggie's stepbrother William and stepsister Ellen. Maggie later wrote that these were the happiest years of her life.

Through J.J.'s mining connections, the Browns began hosting parties in their home. The couple soon became well established in Leadville's social circles, hosting gala balls and social benefits.

In 1891, the Ibex Mining Company was formed by several prominent Leadville mining men, including Eben Smith, August R. Meyer, A.V. Hunter and John F. Campion, friends of J.J. Brown. Campion was well respected for his mining knowledge and was known as "Leadville Johnny." Many historians and writers have often confused J.J. Brown with "Leadville Johnny."

In 1893, Campion hired Brown as superintendent to lead the development of their mines, including one in particular known as the Little Jonny Mine. The silver mine was a rather small producer and had changed owners several times before Campion and his company purchased it. The original discoverer, John F. Johns, named his claim for his son, Johnny. However, the recorded mining claim left off the "h" in "Johnny."

Campion and Brown were well suited to work together. They were the mining men of the next era. The days of surface mining were over. To find the richer ores, mine owners needed to devise ways to dig deeper into the earth. Brown was given the task of finding a way into the depth of the Little Jonny Mine. For the next few years, the two worked together, devising methods, utilizing technology and experimenting.

Brown ordered an additional mine shaft to be dug at the Little Jonny. However, the shaft hit a layer of dolomite sand, which caused the vertical shaft to cave in. Brown's persistence and experimentation paid off. He used bales of hay and added timbers to stabilize the walls of the shaft. The digging continued, eventually pushing through the sand and opening the lower area of the mine. There, a treasure-trove of vast quantities of copper and gold were discovered. Brown and his employers turned the former silver mine into a gold mine, producing more gold than the Leadville area, known for silver, had ever seen.

"LITTLE JONNY STRIKE TO REVIVE LEADVILLE." This was the headline of the *Leadville Herald Democrat* issue of October 29, 1893. The article went on to report that the Little Jonny Mine was shipping over 135 tons of gold ore per day and also stated that Colorado School of Mines' Professor Tilden had visited the mine and declared, "It is practically a lake of ore, with some of the vugs yielding as high as $60 to the pound in gold."

In 1884, the Ibex Mining Company did so well that it paid $1 million in stockholder dividends. Grateful to J.J. Brown, the company awarded him not only his share of the dividend but an additional 12,500 company shares as well.

It was with this newfound wealth that the Browns purchased the mansion on Pennsylvania Avenue and made their permanent move to the state's capital city of Denver.

And the Rest Is History

The Browns made several additions and improvements to their new home. They added a five-foot-tall stone retaining wall to the front of their property, framed with sandstone columns. They also built a sandstone stair walkway to the porch and entrance of the mansion. The porch bannisters were replaced with sandstone columns. The wooden shingle roof was replaced with a fireproof roof, including French tiles. In the back of the home, the two smaller porches were combined into one and enclosed with a new veranda built of brick. The carriage house, located in the rear of the property, was expanded to house several carriages and, eventually, automobiles.

Inside the home, the Browns installed a steam heating system. The radiators were painted in gold and enhanced with hand-painted cupids and fish. The interior was completely redecorated in Maggie's eclectic taste, with added touches insisted by J.J. The entrance hall, elaborately decorated with plaster Nubian slaves and enormous plants, also included a few mounted coyotes. The walls were lined with Victorian decorated wallpaper enhanced by gold-painted trim. In the left corner of the room, a Turkish-style bench placed below the arched window allowed guests to wait before being received by the Browns. A tall wooden stand with a silver bowl allowed visitors to leave their calling cards. The guests would then be received in the parlor. This room also showed Maggie's influence, as well as J.J.'s decorative touch. A large painting depicting the South Platte River with the Rocky Mountain backdrop was placed above the fireplace mantle, and a large polar bear rug lay over the polished wood floor. European art objects would later grace the room, purchased on the Browns' many trips abroad.

The library was decorated with a variety of plants and leather furniture. In the dining room, the Browns added a new marble-topped sideboard, a large dining table and a beautiful china cabinet. In fact, when the Browns left Leadville, they gave nearly all of their furniture to the various members of Maggie's family who remained in Leadville. Maggie's parents soon moved into the mansion, where they would live the remainder of their lives.

Opposite, top: Maggie decorated her home in an eclectic style. *Denver Public Library.*

Opposite, bottom: J.J. and Margaret Tobin Brown with their two children, Lawrence Palmer and Catherine Ellen. *Denver Public Library.*

Settling in Denver, Maggie enrolled her children in the best private schools, while J.J. continued with his mining interests, which required a great deal of traveling across the state. With her husband away, Maggie found the time and independence to involve herself with social and political issues she had long been interested in.

Despite a few of the earlier Brown biographers who embellished Maggie's history and, later, Hollywood's outlandish exaggerations to the contrary, the Browns were accepted in many of Denver's social circles. Denver newspapers covered the Browns' social events in both Leadville and Denver. In fact, the Brown name appeared in the Denver social registries beginning in 1894 and remained in the subsequent registries for the next two decades. Among the first of Denver's social elite to welcome the Browns into Denver society were Mr. and Mrs. James B. Grant, the former governor. One of the first of many articles reporting on the Browns and their social events appeared in the *Denver Times*, which wrote, "Mr. and Mrs. Brown first made their bow to Denver society under the friendly chaperonage of Mrs. J.B. Grant. When the wife of the millionaire mine owner first came to the city it was the Grants who were the first to welcome them. It was in their box at the theater [the Tabor Opera House] that she [Mrs. Brown] was the observed of all observers."

There was an upper-crust self-imposed social set in Denver that disregarded Mr. and Mrs. James J. Brown. Led by Denver's wealthy socialite Mrs. Crawford (Louise Sneed) Hill, the group known as the "Sacred Thirty-Six," considered the Browns newfound wealth to be inferior to their own wealth, either inherited or accumulated over the past few decades since Colorado statehood. The Browns were also Irish Catholics, which was not looked favorably upon in turn-of-the-century Denver. Nevertheless, the Browns were welcomed by much of Denver's society elite, including Edward Wolcott, Colorado's U.S. senator, and Edward P. Costigan, who would later become a U.S. senator, as well as their wives. The Browns were also accepted into the prestigious Denver Country Club.

The Browns held large social dinners and events at their new home. String quartets or bands, depending on the occasion, were often hired to play for the guests from the upper balcony. Among the frequent guests to their home were J.J.'s old friend and business associate A.V. Hunter and his wife; Mr. and Mrs. Peter McCourt, the brother of Mrs. H.A.W. Tabor, better known as Baby Doe Tabor; John Campion; and several local and statewide politicians. The *Denver Times* reported, "Mrs. Brown's vivacity and merry disposition is a most refreshing trait in a society where women of her position, the smart set, any disposition to be natural and animated is quite frowned upon."

Margaret Brown dressed for the opera. *Denver Public Library.*

The Brown home, shortly after Maggie installed the stone lion sculptures. It would be forever known as the "House of Lions." *Denver Public Library.*

When the Brown family returned from Europe, they added their purchases of art, sculptures, tapestries, furniture and rugs to their Denver mansion. Of particular note were four large granite statues of lions, which were placed atop the stone walls in front of the mansion. Interviewed in the Denver papers regarding the lion statuary, Maggie said, "Some people smirked when I brought home ancient statuary from Europe and decorated up a few acres of the Rocky Mountains for my home, but I am sure that those who know the place will agree that culture knows no boundaries and that the fine arts are international." Thus the press dubbed the Brown home the "House of Lions."

In 1898, J.J. Brown suffered a stroke, which left him partially paralyzed for some time. While he eventually recovered, his health was never the same. He and Maggie made significant alterations to their finances, including selling many of his mining interests and transferring ownership of the Pennsylvania Avenue mansion into Maggie's name. Brown's reflections on his recent health scare were detailed in an article in the *Rocky Mountain News*, printed in the July 28, 1899 issue:

> *James J. Brown of the Little Jonny Mine has made up his mind to retire temporarily from the business. This determination was reached through the*

advice of physicians, who tell Mr. Brown that he should separate himself from his affairs and not allow his mind to rest on them. He said his health had not been good, and so long as he stayed in reach of his affairs he could not let them alone. "You see, I have got to take care of myself. My wife owns our residence here, it will not be given up. It is in the nature of a will, though I don't expect to die."

Maggie began to immerse herself in charity work, politics and social causes. She was a strong advocate of women's rights. As a charter member of the Denver Woman's Club, she worked for social justice and equality for women in all social stations in life. She also became associated with newly formed Denver Women's Press Club, established in 1898.

Maggie's Irish Catholic heritage evoked a sense of passion and duty to various Catholic causes in the city. She held several charity events to raise money for St. Joseph's Hospital, including a bazaar held on the lawn of her Denver mansion complete with music, performing clowns and cotton candy. Due to the great success of these events, Maggie was often called on to host charitable events. One such event occurred during the second week of May 1899. The *Denver Times* dated May 12, 1899, covered the event: "Governor Thomas and Mayor Johnson opened the St. Joseph's hospital benefit bazaar at Coliseum hall last night…The moving power in the whole scheme is Mrs. J.J. Brown, the president, whose organization of the various committees who have carried the undertaking up to its present dimensions, has been remarkably successful."

Maggie hosted a few more fundraisers during the summer, which culminated in the July 24, 1899 ceremony at St. Joseph's hospital, laying the new cornerstone for the future west wing.

However, her successful fundraising efforts were overshadowed by the death of her father. Seventy-six-year-old John Tobin died in the Brown mansion on April 20, 1899.

With his wife's submersion in various charitable causes, J.J. was free to spend more time with his mining friends. Not to be outdone by his wife's Denver press coverage, he, too, made the pages of the *Denver Times* on October 11, 1900, where it was reported, "Mr. and Mrs. James J. Brown, formerly of this city and now of Denver, are guests of the Vendome Hotel. Mr. Brown likes to get back to Leadville ever so often and meet his old mining friends. Mining to him is about the best business on earth, and while he does not feel inclined to do any more active mining anymore, he is constantly getting interested in propositions with his old friends."

The Browns returned to their Pennsylvania Street home in time for the winter social events, and their activities were again covered in all the papers. Reporting on one of the many social events, the *Denver Times* of December 9, 1900, said, "The Brown box at the opera [the Tabor Opera House in Denver] was the focus of many opera glasses every night, for the ladies who were Mrs. J.J. Brown's guests included some of the smartest gowned women in Denver. Mrs. Brown's gown was as original as her ideas. The beautiful gold embroidered dress worn at the Silver Slaves' Ball was again a hit at the first night of the opera."

Maggie closed the winter social scene by hosting a Christmas party for the underprivileged children of Denver. Held at the Brown Palace Hotel, the event was complete with Santa Claus, presents and candy. The Browns also sent Christmas gifts to the miners at the Little Jonny Mine in Leadville, a tradition they would continue for years.

Education was very important to Margaret Brown. Following the winter social events of 1900, she took her children to Europe, where she placed Helen in a Paris convent. Returning to the states, she enrolled Lawrence in St. John's College in Fordham, New York. While in New York, at the age of thirty-four, Maggie enrolled at the Carnegie Institute, the first woman to do so. Here, she learned English, French, German and Russian and studied the arts.

In 1903, as Maggie's commitment to social reform grew and as she became deeply involved with the women's suffrage movement, she campaigned for the Colorado State Senate. It was a bold move for a woman, yet Maggie was indeed a bold woman. Many of her Denver friends were taken aback by the action, and even her husband disapproved. Although Maggie didn't win the election, she strongly believed in her convictions, which ultimately led to breaking the barrier of Victorian gender conventions of male dominance.

Due to a difference of opinion regarding Maggie's suffragette activities— or perhaps due to a simple matter of conflicting schedules—the Browns spent the next two years virtually apart. J.J. spent time in the warmer climates of Arizona and California, while Maggie traveled to Newport, Rhode Island, where she spent time with the many friends she had made over the years, including the Vanderbilts and Mr. and Mrs. John Jacob Astor.

By 1906, the Browns were living separately. J.J. could no longer tolerate his wife's suffragist attitude and actions. The lively woman he had married had gained a confident air that was in opposition to J.J.'s conventional concept of a wife. Maggie stayed in the mansion when she was in Denver, while J.J. either traveled or stayed at the Adams Hotel. The couple did their best to keep their marital situation private, but the Denver winds of gossip swirled with speculation. That same year, they privately put their finances in order. Ironically, it wasn't Polly Pry's social gossip paper that eventually broke the story but rather the *Denver Times*. The January 24, 1910 issue ran the headline "The J.J. Browns Divorced." The article read in part:

> *Are the J.J. Browns divorced?*
>
> *J.J. Brown has stated a number of times to the various men about town that the bonds have been severed. Mrs. J.J. Brown has never been approached on the subject, and as she is at present in New York City with her sister, the Countess Von Reitzenstein and her daughter, Miss Helen Brown, the story has not been confirmed by her. However, J.J. Brown, who was in the city a few weeks ago, made no secret of the matter, stating quite positively to certain close friends of his that the decree was signed shortly before Christmas. Of course the report comes as no surprise to Denverites, for it has been an open secret for a year or more that there was anything but harmony reigning in the handsome home on Pennsylvania street.*

In fact, Maggie; her daughter, Helen; and her sister Helen, the Countess Von Reitzenstein, were still in Denver at the Brown home. According to a Margaret Brown biographer, Kristen Iversen, another Denver newspaper, the *Denver Post*, accused the *Denver Times* of "meanness and mendacity." The very next day, in an effort to retract the story, the *Denver Times* actually made the attempt to contact Mrs. Brown. In the following issue of the paper on January 25, 1910, the headline read "Divorce Denied" and included the statement, "Mrs. Brown, who could not be reached yesterday." The article reported, "It now appears through statements of friends of Brown, that the man had been ill for a long time and that his malady is the cause of certain rash announcements that have no foundation."

The article continued, "Mrs. Brown herself says that she and her husband are separated, although not legally." Mrs. Brown was quoted as saying, "In the face of our Catholic religion, we could not think of divorce." As devout Catholics, they never divorced, but their subsequent separation, now very public, was swift and final. The Browns privately signed a legal separation agreement, after twenty-three years of marriage. According to the agreement, dated August 10, 1909, Margaret received a cash settlement, stocks and dividends and a $700 monthly living expense. She also maintained possession of the Pennsylvania Street mansion, which had been signed over to her in 1898.

Margaret Brown, circa 1910. *Denver Public Library.*

Now more independent than ever, Maggie rented out her Denver mansion and found solace with her friends in the East, at Newport Beach, where she rented a fashionable cottage. Following the Christmas holiday season of 1911, Maggie was invited to join a group of friends including Mr. and Mrs. John Jacob Astor IV on a tour of the Middle East. The group left New York Harbor on January 25, 1912, traveling through the Indian Ocean and arriving in Cairo, Egypt, where Helen joined her mother. After several days in Egypt, the traveling party left for Paris in early April 1912.

At the hotel in Paris, Maggie received an urgent cable from her son in the States informing her that her grandson, Lawrence Brown Jr., was gravely ill. Originally, Maggie had planned to stay in Paris a while with Helen, and the Astors would travel back to New York on the maiden voyage of the world's largest ship, the RMS *Titanic*, lauded as the finest ocean ship in the world. At the last minute, Astor was able to book passage for Maggie as well. The ship, advertised as "practically unsinkable," left the port of Cherbourg, France, in the English Channel, at 8:00 p.m. on April 10, 1912. It would never make it to the harbors of New York City.

The *Titanic* represented the newest technology, a wonder of modern science in an era of transatlantic travel. Built by Harland and Wolff of Belfast, Ireland, the ship was designed by Thomas Andrews for the White Star Lines, at a cost of $10 million. The enormous vessel weighed forty-six thousand tons and was 882.5 feet long.

Maggie enjoyed herself with all the celebrations on board the *Titanic*'s first voyage. She dined with the Astors, Mr. and Mrs. Benjamin Guggenheim, Captain Smith and J. Bruce Ismay, the owner of the White Star Line.

As the ship traveled west through the cold north Atlantic Ocean, the ship's captain and crew received numerous telegraph warnings of ice in the area near Nova Scotia. Nevertheless, at 11:40 p.m. on April 14, 1912, the *Titanic* struck the edge of an iceberg. Distress signals were immediately sent out, but it was apparent the *Titanic* would sink. Within an hour, at 12:45 a.m., the first lifeboat was lowered into the freezing waters of the Atlantic Ocean. At 12:55 a.m., Maggie was ordered into lifeboat #6, which included twenty women, two men and a young boy.

Maggie's heroics in the face of disaster as the great ship *Titanic* sank are only downplayed by Maggie herself. While Maggie loved to tell the tall tale now and again, she very rarely discussed the tragic event or her part in organizing the survivors and the ultimate rescue. During that fateful hour when it was determined that the ship would indeed sink, Maggie diligently prepared. She dressed in several layers and took nothing with her but the cash she had.

Concerned for several hysterical women hovering on the deck, Maggie gently encouraged them toward the lowering lifeboats before she herself got into one. Maggie calmed the women by shedding her layers of clothing to keep them warm. She encouraged them to row away from the sinking ship.

In the darkness, with the stars dancing brightly overhead, Maggie and the group in lifeboat #6 watched as the great ship slowly sank into the sea. It was 2:30 a.m. As the ship was sinking, hundreds of people jumped off or were thrust into the icy ocean. The horrific screams could be heard across the freezing waters as the lifeboats rowed away. Maggie insisted they go back to rescue the helpless, but one of the two men on the lifeboat, the *Titanic*'s quartermaster, Robert Hitchens, refused. After six hours of constant rowing, the lights of the SS *Carpathia* came into view, and rescue was at hand.

Safely aboard the *Carpathia*, Maggie immediately sent a wire to her son letting him know she was safe. Maggie then began to speak with and console survivors, many of whom spoke very little English. Because she knew several languages, Maggie was able to converse with many of the rescued passengers. Following the rescue, Maggie's true character and compassion was finally exposed to all the world. With newspaper reporters and photographers hounding her, she bellowed, "Leave me alone! I have work to do. People need me. Come back later." And they did. When the *Carpathia* finally docked at New York's Pier 54, a crowd of nearly thirty thousand people were waiting to greet the survivors of the horrific tragedy of the century. Mrs. Margaret Tobin Brown was singled out among the survivors by the many local and national reporters and photographers. When asked why she thought she had survived the disaster, in her characteristic wit, Maggie replied, "Typical Brown luck. We're unsinkable."

Reporters from all the Denver newspapers hung out at the Brown Palace asking for interviews with Mrs. Brown. She refused all interviews. Frustrated reporters pressed her for an account of the tragedy. In the April 30, 1912 issue of the *Denver Post*, Maggie replied to one reporter, "Will I do it? No. I don't mind telling things I know to people I am sure are deeply interested in it." She eventually gave an interview to the *Denver Times*.

The city of Denver welcomed the heroine of the *Titanic* with open arms. Even Mrs. Crawford Hill of the social elite group the Sacred Thirty-Six welcomed Maggie with a luncheon at the Denver Country Club. The *Rocky Mountain News* issue of May 2, 1912, reported on the affair, commenting:

> *Thus has the "thirty-six" vindicated itself and proved that the open sesame to its sacred circles is neither money nor social prestige; that a splendid*

action calls forth a quick response from the impulsive leader of that small and exclusive portion of society. It is a universal ambition almost, among women, to be in "the social swim," but it seems strange that to Mrs. Brown, out of the terrible night of suffering, hardship and death should come that great prize—admission to exclusive society.

Maggie resumed her interests in the social issues of the day, particularly concerning women and children. In April 1914, Maggie boldly stepped into the middle of Colorado's largest labor war.

The miners at the Colorado Fuel and Iron Company, part of John D. Rockefeller's industrial empire, had been on strike since the previous winter. In retaliation, the miners were evicted from their company homes near Trinidad. Undaunted, they set up the tent colony known as Ludlow, with over two hundred tents and nearly one thousand people. Under the guidance of the United Mine Workers of America, their demands were for an eight-hour work schedule, decent living accommodations and safe working conditions. The company held firm and refused to negotiate. Former governor James B. Grant, united with the American Smelter and Refining Company, backed the mine owners.

As tension mounted, Governor Elias M. Ammons sent the Colorado National Guard to the area. To the miners, this only escalated the tension. On the morning of April 20, 1914, shots were fired, though no one knows to this day which side fired first. The Colorado militia released bombs into the tent colony and opened fire on the miners. The miners retaliated with their own gunfire. The battle raged for fourteen long hours. When it was over, twenty-five people were dead, including two women and eleven children. The April 21, 1914 issue of the *Trinidad Chronicle News* carried the devastation under the headline "25 DEAD, 3 WOUNDED. TENT COLONY SWEPT OUT OF EXISTENCE."

Colorado citizens learned of the horrifying details of the "Ludlow Massacre" on the front page of nearly every newspaper. One of the most violent labor conflicts in American history, it stirred outrage across America. Maggie was among those outraged citizens. From Denver, she immediately arranged for food, clothing, shoes and blankets to be sent to the surviving families at Ludlow. She then traveled to Ludlow, where, after surveying the scene of carnage, she helped the Red Cross by recruiting nurses. With Maggie's mining connections across the state, many from both sides of the labor issue saw her as an ally.

Back in Denver, Maggie appealed to various women's groups, and together they raised money for the victims and brought awareness of the labor problem to the forefront. Her efforts helped to bring reform and change in Colorado's labor laws.

That same summer, Maggie had launched her campaign for congress in her Denver district. Running on a platform of equal rights, she was one of the first women in the state to do so. However, as summer came to a close, she withdrew from the race, as reported in the *Rocky Mountain News* on August 12, 1914, which stated, "Mrs. J.J. Brown of Denver and Newport will abandon her campaign for congress—this year at least. She wired State Senator Helen Ring Robinson yesterday that she could not attend the congressional primaries, having reached the conclusion that this was no time for Colorado to change congressmen."

Maggie later launched a campaign for U.S. senator in Colorado. However, when America entered World War I, Maggie abandoned her political aspirations for the cause she really believed in: alleviating human suffering. Her son, Lawrence, had joined the U.S. Army, and Maggie felt duty-bound to do her part. She offered her Newport cottage to the American Red Cross, which used it as a satellite hospital for the U.S. Navy. She focused on relief efforts, traveling to France to work for the American Committee for Devastated France. Maggie earned the French Legion of Honor for her activities. She was later received in the White House by President Calvin Coolidge.

On September 5, 1922, sixty-eight-year-old James Joseph Brown died after a long illness in Hempstead, Long Island, New York, where he was living with his daughter, Mrs. George Benziger. The *Leadville Herald Democrat* reported the death: "A telegram announcing the death in Hempstead, N.Y. of James J. Brown was received by J.K. Brown, 115 East Eighth Street, a relative, yesterday. As far as is known, Mr. Brown's only relatives in this city at present are J.K. Brown and his sons, Edward and James Brown, and Miss Minnie Brown."

Unfortunately, he had not left a legal will, which resulted in family tension and, eventually, court fights. After years of litigation, which pitted Maggie against her children, the estate was settled in 1927. Maggie received half of the estate and all of J.J.'s mining shares. The remaining half of the estate was split equally between the two Brown children. Maggie left the Denver courthouse for a long vacation, while the children made derogatory comments in the press about their mother, with Helen even saying she never cared to see her mother again. When Maggie read the comments in the newspapers, she rewrote her own will, leaving both children out.

As Maggie spent most of her time in Newport, in 1911 she rented out her Denver mansion to the Cosgriff family. When they moved into their new home on Grant Street, Maggie rented the mansion to the Keiser family. When the Keiser family moved out, they took with them the original library cases, apparently purchased from Maggie. The mansion was then rented to Lucille Hubbel. In 1926, Maggie was forced to take legal action, evicting Hubbel for subletting rooms.

The era of the Great Depression affected the nation's economy and caused extreme hardship to millions of Americans. Maggie was forced to give up her Newport cottage, living in local hotels. She managed to hang on to her Denver mansion by turning it into a boardinghouse for added income, under the direction of her trusted housekeeper, Ella Grable.

Living in New York in 1931, Maggie had a suite at the Barbizon Plaza Hotel, a fashionable women's hotel known for hosting the wealthy and famous, including Hollywood actress Ingrid Bergman. Here, Maggie continued with her activist activities and spent social time with her friends on the eastern seaboard. While staying at the hotel, Maggie suffered two strokes, and on October 26, 1932, at the age of sixty-five, Maggie died in her sleep.

The death of the iconic *Titanic* survivor was front-page news across the world. The *Denver Post* eulogized, "A career as colorful, dramatic and inspiring as a western sunset came to an abrupt close. She was a definite, fearless personality. She knew what she wanted and went after it, and seldom failed in her goal."

Maggie's daughter, Helen, made the funeral arrangements and burial followed in the Holy Rood Cemetery on New York's Long Island, where she was buried next to her husband. Maggie's will revealed that she had overcome the hard feelings of ten years ago. Her son and daughter were the primary beneficiaries of her estate.

Because of the depressed economy during the 1930s, the House of Lions was worth a fraction of what the Browns had paid for it in 1894. In an effort to liquidate, Maggie's children auctioned off the furnishings to pay off the remaining $3,000 mortgage. They then sold their family home to Jay Weatherly in 1933 for $5,000.

The mansion had suffered from neglect for years and was in disrepair. Weatherly took on the task of restoring and remodeling the former Brown home into a rooming house with twelve rooms.

Over the next two decades, ownership of the mansion changed several times, as did both the exterior and interior of the "Denver showplace," as the *Rocky Mountain News* once called it. In 1958, Art Leisenring bought the mansion, turning it into a gentlemen's boardinghouse. He knew the history of the home and attempted to garner interest from the City of Denver for restoration. Unable to persuade the city officials, in 1960 he leased the home to—ironically enough—the city's juvenile court system—a cause Margaret Brown had long championed—which used it as a home for troubled young girls. By the 1960s and the new era of "Urban Renewal," the home was scheduled for demolition.

It was a remarkable oversight by Denver officials. Over the years, Maggie's story had been told and retold in magazines and books and even on the radio, featuring Hollywood movie star Helen Hayes. Her story of rags to riches and courage in the face of the *Titanic* tragedy took on a life of its own. The truth was embellished, and several accounts—pure fiction—were written simply to sell the story. Gene Fowler's bestseller, *Timberline*, written just two years after Maggie's death, was one of the first published materials referring to Margaret Tobin Brown as "Molly." The name stuck in popular culture from then on. In 1960, the stage play *The Unsinkable Molly Brown* appeared on Broadway to rave reviews. Staring Tammy Grimes, the play was such a hit in New York that it became a national sensation. The play crossed the nation from New York City to Denver to the West Coast, with nearly two thousand sell-out crowds. This was followed later that same year by Hollywood's movie version of the same title, starring Debbie Reynolds. The legend of Molly Brown was a sensation in 1960 pop culture.

Still, the city of Denver paid little attention. It was the era of the city's Urban Renewal Project, and many historic Denver structures were destroyed to make way for parking lots and modern buildings. In 1970, the former Brown home was set for demolition. In an effort to save the historic residence, Christine Kosewick wrote an impassioned letter to Colorado's first lady Ann Love. Mrs. Love then contacted a few people who might be willing to help. This led to a formation of concerned citizens who created Historic Denver, Inc. Through its fundraising efforts, the group was able to purchase the House of Lions in 1971, the home of the *Titanic*'s most famous survivor, for $80,000, saving it from demolition. This was the first in a long series of historic preservation projects that Historic Denver, Inc., would be credited for saving.

Today

Historic Denver, Inc., began the restoration process of the Brown mansion to its former "showplace" in the days when the Browns called it home. The

Molly Brown House. *Linda Wommack.*

goal was to open the home as a museum. Using architectural research, paint-chip analysis and original photographs taken in 1910—thanks to the foresight of Maggie—the home was restored to the time period of the early twentieth century.

The only change needed to the exterior of the property was to repaint the wooden trim in the salmon color the Browns used in 1910. Extensive landscaping was required to return the lawns to their appearance shown in photographs. The interior of the residence was an entirely different matter. Over the many years, the floors had sustained considerable damage from neglect. A few of the wooden floors had been covered for years with old carpet or re-floored, and others were covered in linoleum. Several of the walls had been stripped of the original wallpaper and either painted, replastered or wallpapered again. During the restoration, the added walls and changes to the rooms in the 1930s were brought back to the original house design. When this was completed, the original wooden floors were refurbished and walls were restored with fresh paint, while others were covered with wallpaper matching as closely as possible the 1910 photographs, complete with the gold-painted trim. The oak staircases, with the machine-turned spindles, were also restored to their natural look. The furniture placed throughout the mansion is a collection of Victorian-era pieces and artwork and furniture actually owned by the Browns, located after an extensive search by members of Historic Denver, Inc.

Today, the Brown mansion is open to the public as the Molly Brown House Museum. Visitors to Maggie's former home will walk through the rooms that Maggie walked through and called home.

Entering the museum through the front porch, where the original tile floor remains, to the left of the entry hall is the original Turkish-style corner and the bench installed below the window.

On the main floor, the library includes the original bookcases, remarkably returned to the home after being sold in 1918. The dining room is also restored to its original state, including the unusual combed plaster walls. This room displays an elegant punch bowl, a carving set and a silver soup tureen, all possessions of the Browns.

The second floor offers a glimpse of the personal lives of the Browns, including the individual bedrooms of the Brown family members, the children and Maggie's parents. The Tobin Room, named for Maggie's parents, includes several family photos and personal possessions of Maggie's, such as plaster vases and oil paintings, received as wedding gifts.

Margaret Tobin Brown, the "Unsinkable," was truly a lady ahead of her time. Her flamboyant, independent nature paved the way for generations of women. Her rags-to-riches life and her legendary heroics have left us with a yarn of myth and mystique spun around a grand lady that will forever be unsinkable.

Fun Facts

- When the Browns purchased the newest of modern technology, the hand-crank telephone, their exchange was A-1466.
- The first moving pictures of the *Titanic*, taken minutes before it left the port, arrived in Denver on April 23, 1912. Denverites flocked to the local theaters to see the film coverage.
- Lawrence Brown eventually moved to Leadville, where he served as a director of the Ibex Mining Company. He died in Leadville in 1949. Helen Brown Benziger lived long enough to see her mother's life

portrayed on both the Broadway stage and in Hollywood film. She died in 1969.

- Despite the wishes of both J.J. and Maggie to be buried in Colorado, James Joseph Brown and Margaret Tobin Brown are buried in the Holy Rood Cemetery on New York's Long Island. Each of their etched-in-stone tombstones give incorrect birth dates. J.J. Brown's birth date reads 1855, when, in fact, it was 1854, and Maggie's reads 1868, which was actually 1864.
- The Molly Brown House was placed on the National Register on February 2, 1972, 5DV.178.

Contact Information

THE BROWN HOUSE MUSEUM
1340 Pennsylvania Street
Denver, Colorado 80203
www.mollybrown.org
(303) 832-4092

Chapter 5

THE WILBER S. RAYMOND HOUSE/CASTLE MARNE—DENVER—1889

A SLEEPING BEAUTY

The Beginning

The city of Denver benefited from the financial boom brought from the state's mining industry. Sixteenth Street became known as the "Wall Street of the West." Following the rich discovery of silver high in the Rocky Mountains near Leadville, a new economic boom trickled throughout the state, and Denver's economy soared.

In 1887, the Denver real estate firm of Porter, Raymond & Company began the development of some of Capitol Hill's finest residential areas. This land was originally owned by Elias G. Mathem, who purchased it on July 12, 1866. For the next two decades, the land was prime farmland, with water supplied by the Smith's Ditch in 1867. With the economic boom of the 1880s, Mathem saw his chance for a huge return on his investment. He recorded his land as a residential plat on August 30, 1880. He sold the now platted land parcel to George Fryer on December 8, 1880. Fryer had made several rich ore discoveries in Leadville, where Fryer Hill was named in his honor. Fryer then sold the land for $3,000 to John H. Wyman, a New York real estate investor who had arrived in the young city in 1866. Wyman's intent for his new purchase of land, located two miles east of Denver City, was also as residential development. However, there was no interest in the large parcel of grassy wind-blown prairie so far from Denver's downtown business district.

When Wyman sold the land to Porter, Raymond & Company, he enjoyed a high profit for his original $3,000 investment, selling the land for $300,000. Access to the once-remote area changed with the advent of electric streetcar rails in 1889.

The real estate investment company, consisting of brothers Isham B. and William W. Porter, along with Charles A. Raymond, launched a massive marketing campaign of the new Capitol Hill neighborhood, called Wyman's Addition. Through their promotion, they were able to attract several of Denver's wealthy citizens to build their homes in the new residential community. Charles A. Raymond was the first to build his fine mansion at the southeast corner of Colfax Avenue and Race Street. He was soon followed by his relative Wilbur S. Raymond, a banking investor who turned to real estate investments during the great economic boom in the city.

Glory Days

Wilbur S. Raymond purchased lots in the Wyman district at the corner of Sixteenth Avenue and Race Street for $15,000. In 1889, he hired Denver's most popular architect, William Lang, to build his home. Lang began his storied career in Denver in 1886. Lang and his partner, Marshall Pugh, had previously built a town hall, an apartment house, a courthouse, a church and a large business block in downtown Denver. Located at Seventeenth and Champa Streets, a three-story commercial building, known as the Ghost Block, was the only commercial building Lang constructed in Denver. It was an impressive résumé, which must have intrigued W.S. Raymond. Lang's plans for the Raymonds' mansion were immediately approved, and construction began that year.

The *Denver Republican* newspaper dated January 1, 1890, reported on the new "show home" being built. The article went on to say, "The fact that men are able to build and maintain such houses and the further fact that they possess the taste for these elegant domestic surroundings, proves to the world that Denver has reached the social age in which refinement, culture and love of the beautiful stamp the character of the people."

Following the completion of the Raymond home, an article appeared in an 1890 issue of the *Western Architect and Building News*. The article featured Lang's many works. Prominent in the piece was the "Raymond house on the corner of 16th and Race Streets," referring to the edifice as "one of Lang's larger stone houses."

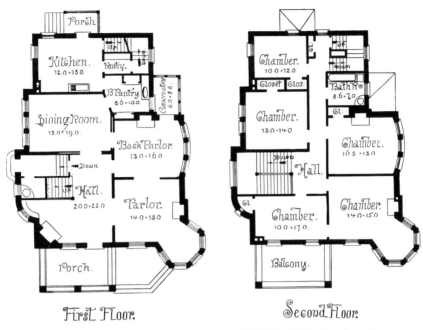

RESIDENCE OF W. S. RAYMOND, ESQ., DENVER, COLO.—See Page 33.

The original blueprints of the Raymond home, later known as Castle Marne. *Denver Public Library.*

Raymond and his family moved into the $40,000 "show home" later that year. It was indeed a spectacular residence. The Raymonds' new manor, built in the Richardsonian Romanesque style, was constructed entirely of rough-hewn native lava stone, a trademark of Lang's work. The quarried stone—purchased in Castle Rock, Colorado, and composed mainly of quartz, mica and feldspar—added sparkle and glitter to the stone mansion on bright sunny days.

Lang added a unique aspect to the exterior stonework, a style unknown in Denver at the time, which he also used in designing the similar mansion on Pennsylvania Avenue, later owned by J.J. and Margaret "Molly" Brown. It was a style of decorative masonry known as "rustication," achieved by cutting back the edges of stones to a plane surface while leaving the central portion of the stone in its natural rough or projected state. This style of masonry lent a bold surface to the exterior of the mansion's stone walls. Indiana rhyolite trim graced the native stone.

This early photo of Castle Marne shows what is believed to be the Raymond family on the porch. *Denver Public Library.*

The exterior of the mansion, with its eyebrow dormers, hand-hewn cornices, rounded arches and towers, reflected the eclecticism associated with Lang's work. The asymmetrical massing was lavishly enhanced by Lang's elaborate displays of carved stonework and featured rich detailing throughout the three-story edifice.

The entry to the mansion included a mounting stone at the street edge, allowing for the ease of visitors disembarking from their carriages. A hitching post was also available. The portico was graced with matching rough stone columns supporting the arched parlor window on the second floor, above the entry.

The steep-pitched roof, with nine fluted chimneys, included a distinct corner chimney. There were several additional signature traits of Lang's work, such as turrets, in the exterior of the mansion, complemented with carved stone filigrees. Another feature was the prominent five-sided corner tower on the south side of the residence. Lang was also fond of round windows, often cutting off the bottom curve so that the glass resembled the sun just dipping below the horizon.

On the north side, Lang showed off his typical stone detail by including a round stained-glass window above two arched columns framed in carved rhyolite trim. Three native-stone balustrades supported the southwest porch. One of the balustrades included an intricately carved display of lotus plants. A nineteenth-century symbol of welcome, the lotus plant was carved in three stages of growth continuing up the balustrade. At the bottom was the lotus plant, halfway up was the lotus bud and near the top was the lotus bloom.

A low retaining wall, also made of native stone, surrounded much of the property. Behind the mansion, on the southeast lot of the property, a carriage house was constructed in matching native-stone materials. Trees were planted, and landscaping included bushes and climbing vines, which would eventually reach the roof of the five-sided corner tower.

The beautiful black oak front door, trimmed in matching dark oak and complete with a buzzer, alerted the staff to visitors. Inside the Raymond home, twenty-two-inch-thick stone walls contained thirty-one rooms. Ten- to twelve-foot ceilings graced many of the large rooms. Raymond's home was one of the first in the Wyman neighborhood to include indoor plumbing. The home also featured both electric and gas lighting, as the new innovative electric lighting system was somewhat unreliable.

Visitors entering the home were received in the imposing foyer with extravagant oak woodwork. An ornately carved fireplace, to the left of the entrance, featured a beveled round mirror, flat at the bottom, in keeping with Lang's decorative style. The grand oak staircase, with its magnificent horseshoe opening and enhanced with Victorian oak accents, led to the second and third floors. The second entrance to the home, with intricate stone carvings above the door, faced Sixteenth Avenue and led directly to Raymond's private office in the basement of his home, complete with a large fireplace.

The large parlor to the right of the entrance foyer was lavish in design and décor and featured a fireplace with an elaborate carved mahogany mantel. At each end of the mantle was a pair of serpent-like dolphins, a Celtic reference of welcome. The Celtic consort of Mother Earth and the Green Man who guarantees the renewal of the earth, elaborately carved in oak, also graced the fireplace. Other fireplaces throughout the home included intricate tile work and were enhanced with large mirrors as part of the mantels.

The large dining room was stunning with paneled walls of quarter-sawn oak and imported Lincrustra wallcovering from England.

Above: Designed by Denver artist Frank M. Watkins, this six-foot window, known as the "peacock window," depicts flowers and filigree. It is a fine example of the impressionist movement in stained glass. *Castle Marne.*

Right: W.S. Raymond built his home in the new Wyman neighborhood of Denver in 1893. *Denver Public Library.*

94

Among the many intricate details of this home was the wood fretwork incorporated to enhance the windows and doors. Several styles were ordered from the firm of Moses Ransom & Company in Pennsylvania and were used throughout the home.

At the southwest corner of the parlor and the base of the Queen Ann tower was a Turkish-styled nook with large windows gracing the curved area. Tradition holds that this was a variation of the eighteenth-century "widow's walk." The lady of the house would relax in this area while keeping a watchful eye for her husband to return home.

Several stained-glass windows graced the mansion, including a beautiful round window featured on the second-floor staircase landing. A true work of art, it is known as the "peacock window." Designed by Denver artist Frank M. Watkins, the six-foot window depicting flowers and filigree is a fine example of the impressionist movement in stained glass.

The grand staircase continued to the third floor, with a magnificent wide turn in polished oak, allowing for women's sweeping ball gowns to clear the turn unencumbered. The third floor of the castle contained a large ballroom with an eighteen-foot ceiling and polished oak floors. A fireplace heated the room during winter entertainment, and a balcony allowed for guests to retreat for fresh air in the summer.

The Raymond family enjoyed their new home for nearly a year. However, in 1891, Wilbur S. Raymond, heavily in debt, was forced into foreclosure.

And the Rest Is History

The mansion went through several illustrious owners throughout its storied history. Colonel James H. Platt and his wife, the former Sarah Sophia Chase, purchased the mansion in 1892. Platt was born in Canada in 1837 to American parents. Educated in Canada, he later attended the University of Vermont. He served with distinction in the Union army during the Civil War, rising to the rank of colonel before the war's end. Following the war, Platt remained in the military for several years. He was later appointed to serve in President Ulysses S. Grant's cabinet.

Colonel Platt and his wife, Sarah, moved to Denver in 1887, where he served as president of the Equitable Accident Insurance Company. In 1890, he established what would become the finest paper mill in the country. The Denver Paper Mills Company was located in South Denver, at South

Jason Street and Louisiana Avenue, along the South Platte River, an area later known as the Ruby Hill neighborhood. It was an ideal location, with sufficient water and transportation services. The South Park Railroad served the area and provided switch cars that could be loaded or unloaded at the mill. When the mill facilities were completed, at a cost of $575,000, Platt's business complex was the largest in Colorado.

Over 1,200 Denver citizens left Union Station in thirteen Union Pacific railroad cars for the South Denver area and Manchester to see the new factory and attend the grand opening celebration, held on August 23, 1891. During the ceremony, several city and state politicians were present and gave speeches, praising Denver's newest business venture and the new opportunities for employment. Colonel Platt, in his speech to the crowd, said, "Next to Denver's great smelters, the successful establishment of cotton, iron, woolen and paper mills are of the greatest importance to the rapid and permanent growth of our city. We have one of the largest and finest modern paper mills ever constructed in this or any other country."

The *Rocky Mountain News* reported the event in its August 23, 1891 issue with the headline "Paper Now King."

Colonel Platt and his wife were very active in the community. He donated land for parks, including Platt Park and the South Denver housing development, which became known as the Platt Park neighborhood. Sarah focused her attention on the welfare of women and children. Through her tireless work, she became highly respected across the state, eventually becoming the first woman appointed to the Civil Service Commission of Colorado. As such, she was responsible for many of the legal reforms affecting women and children in Colorado. During the economic depression in 1893, following the government's repeal of the Sherman Silver Purchase Act, Sarah Platt organized a large relief effort for the miners and other workers particularly hard hit by the depression. Her local influence in the community grew. She became the first woman to serve on the state board of prisons. She was later elected as the first president of the Denver Women's Club and became national president of the Federation of Associated Women's Clubs.

In June 1894, the Platt family took a fishing vacation at Green Lake, near Georgetown, Colorado. While boating alone on the lake on June 13, 1894, Colonel James H. Platt fell into the water and drowned. He was fifty-seven years old. In June 1895, his widow, Mrs. Sarah Decker Platt, sold the mansion to John T. Mason.

Born in Lincolnshire, England, in 1853, Mason eventually immigrated to America, where he made his way to Houston, Texas. There, he founded a

Colonel James H. Platt and his wife, the former Sarah Sophia Chase, purchased the mansion in 1892. *Denver Public Library.*

chain of mercantile stores. Houston's Mason Park would later be named in his honor. In 1892, Mason and his wife, Francis Schaffter Mason, moved to Denver in an effort to relieve her tubercular condition.

A longtime collector of butterflies and moths, Mason's collection of several thousand specimens soon caught the attention of enthusiasts across the country. The idea for a natural history museum in Denver was first proposed by Breckenridge pioneer Edwin Carter in 1892. By 1899, the city of Denver accepted the proposal. Carter's entire collection of birds and animals, displayed in Breckenridge for years, was the nucleus of the proposed museum, founded on December 6, 1900. Henry M. Porter, an early Denver pioneer and a wealthy Denver businessman, was one of the first Denver citizens to back what would become the Denver Museum of Natural History. Others followed, including John T. Mason and John F. Campion. Mason donated much of his butterfly and moth collection, and Campion donated his impressive collection of gold specimens from mines in the Breckenridge area. When the new museum finally opened in 1908, Mason became the first curator.

In 1911, Frances Schaffter Mason died of tuberculosis. The following year, fifty-nine-year-old-widower John T. Mason married thirty-seven-year-old Dora Porter. Miss Porter was the daughter of Henry M. Porter, with whom Mason had a relationship through the museum venture. As a wedding present to his bride, Mason presented her with the famed Isabella jewels. He had previously purchased the jewels from the estate of Elizabeth "Baby Doe" Tabor at an auction held on the front steps of the International Trust Bank in December 1907.

The jewels had come into the bank's possession when the widow of Horace Austin Warner Tabor (Baby Doe) had used them as collateral for an $8,000 loan, which was never satisfied. The six jewels were exquisite in size and color, ranging from seven to eight carats, including some set into a diamond-studded bracelet. The largest jewel in the collection was a nine-carat diamond, pure white in color. It is said this was the jewel Queen Isabella had sold to finance the exploration for Christopher Columbus's exploration to the New World. The *Rocky Mountain News* reported the details of the auction in the December 17, 1907 issue, describing the jewels as "variously valued from $25,000 to $50,000." Auctioneer and banker John W. Springer accepted the three bids, with the winning bid—an incredibly low $8,007—being awarded to John T. Mason.

Following the wedding, the Mason couple settled into Denver society and was involved in several social and civic issues in the city. Well respected for their efforts and generosity, the Masons' name would later be included in the list of Denver's benefactors on the marble wall of the Greek Amphitheater in Denver's Civic Center Park.

John and Dora Mason sold their Denver home, moving to California in 1918. John T. Mason died in December 1928. Shortly after her husband's death, Mrs. Dora Mason returned to Denver, where she joined her father in establishing the Porter Hospital in southeast Denver. In 1940, she provided the funds for the construction of Mason Hall at the Denver Museum of Natural Science, the former Denver Museum of Natural History, which displayed her husband's enormous moth and butterfly collection.

Mrs. Adele Van Cise purchased the Race Street property from the Masons. She was the widow of Edwin Van Cise, a prominent Denver attorney and chairman of the Denver Public Utilities Commission, who died in 1914. Prior to the Van Cises' move to Denver, they lived in South Dakota, where Edwin Van Cise served as one of the prosecuting attorneys during the trials following the massacre at Wounded Knee on December 29, 1890. Their son, Philip, born on October 25, 1884, in South Dakota, later became a prominent attorney in his own right, graduating from the University of

Philip S. Van Cise, the son of Adele Van Cise, inspired the name of his mother's home, Castle Marne, following his experiences in France during World War I. *Denver Public Library.*

Colorado in 1907 and receiving his law degree in 1909. From 1910 to 1914, he was a member of the Colorado National Guard, eventually attaining the rank of captain. During World War I, he served as an intelligence officer for the United States Army in France, where he served with distinction, receiving the rank of lieutenant colonel.

In 1918, during the height of World War I, Mrs. Adele Van Cise began converting her new home into an eight-unit apartment house. The once-elegant parlor and dining room were subdivided to provide separate apartments on the first floor. Although it was quite an extensive remodeling project, Mrs. Van Cise kept many of the original architectural elements of the castle intact as much as possible and even followed many of the same patterns in the wall décor. Unfortunately, much of the original interlocking spiral moldings along the doors and windows were lost in the new remodeling. Each apartment had a private bathroom and a kitchen. The carriage house was also converted into an apartment.

Returning home following his war experiences in France, Philip Van Cise suggested that his mother rename the home the Marne Apartments, after the many castles he had seen along the Marne River.

In 1921, Philip Van Cise was elected to the office of Denver district attorney. During his tenure, he was responsible for breaking up the crime element in Denver, beginning with Lou Blonger, Denver's underworld boss, and his "Million-Dollar Bunco Ring." Van Cise arrested and successfully prosecuted Blonger in Colorado's longest and most expensive trial at that time. Lou Blonger and twenty of his associates were convicted and sent to prison.

Next, Van Cise took on the Ku Klux Klan. With several members of the Klan holding city and state offices, it was a bold step for Van Cise. Governor Clarence J. Morley, elected in 1925, bowed to the Klan pressure, allowing Grand Dragon Dr. John Locke to hold tight control of Morley's politics and his government. Denver's mayor, Benjamin F. Stapleton, was also a Klan supporter. Several bills were introduced in the senate to abolish and re-create state agencies based on Klan motives. Van Cise eventually prosecuted Locke for tax evasion and sent him to prison in 1926. With the conviction of Colorado's leader of the Ku Klux Klan, Van Cise effectively caused the fall of the Klan influence in the state, almost as suddenly as it had emerged. The political dominoes soon fell. Governor Morley's personal secretary was indicted for mail fraud, two of Locke's advisors went to prison for embezzlement and Morley was defeated in the following election. Shortly thereafter, Morley was convicted of mail fraud and served five years at Leavenworth, the only governor of Colorado to be sent to prison.

Mrs. Adele Van Cise lived in one of the converted apartments of the Marne Apartments until her death in 1937. Following her death, Adele Van Cise's daughter, Ethel, sold the historic edifice to Lyle A. Holland and his wife, Gladys, in 1938. A Denver real estate promoter, Holland managed the apartment complex while living and conducting his real estate business at Castle Marne. For the many years he lived at the historic castle, Holland used the carriage house as a workshop where he also stored his extensive gun collection. Lyle A. Holland lived in the home until his death in 1971. Legend has it that handlers of Holland's estate facilitated the sale of the castle to none other than L. Ron Hubbard, the founder of Scientology. The real estate transaction was ultimately reversed for undisclosed reasons.

Richard and Louise Dice purchased the property in 1974 for $350,000. Although the couple never lived in the historic structure, they originally envisioned converting the mansion into three condominiums, one on each floor of the historic structure. A preliminary business prospectus included the following observation: "From time to time, pieces of architecture are built that have such character and fortitude that they survive through the decades of changes in ownership, changes in the surrounding environment and neighborhoods, various uses and misuses, and still emerge intact, with grace and splendor. Such a structure is the house at 1572 Race."

Unfortunately, Denver's economy suffered during this time as gas and oil prices in America rose sharply. The Dices were not able to attract the businesses they had hoped for and that their business prospectus had envisioned. From 1979 through 1982, the building served as offices on the first and second floors, while the manager's offices were located on the third floor. Businesses operating on the first and second floors included a processing center for parolees from state penal institutions and an anarchist newspaper.

Richard and Louise Dice separated the carriage house property from the Castle Marne property, eventually selling both pieces of property. Castle Marne was sold to local real estate developers for $184,500, while the carriage house was ultimately sold to two young graphic art designers for $165,000.

For the next seven years, the structure sat vacant, a sad sight compared to its past splendor. The new owners turned off the gas and electricity to save money but neglected to turn off the water. The building was constantly vandalized. Anything of historic value was stolen.

Once the show home of the Wyman neighborhood, the historic Castle Marne became known in the area as the "big empty stone house with the beautiful window." Neighbors in the Wyman district thought the house was haunted and would often cross the street rather than walk by the mansion.

The historic home was purchased on August 1, 1988, by James and Diane Peiker. A Colorado native, Jim Peiker grew up in south Denver. Peiker, a former salesman, along with his daughter, Melissa Feher-Peiker, envisioned their "Castle Marne" as a bed-and-breakfast inn in the historic Wyman neighborhood. Because of the dilapidated condition of the edifice, the Peikers continued to look at other properties in the area, but they kept coming back to Castle Marne. Melissa Feher-Peiker, in a conversation with the author, said, "It was serendipity. The house picked us." The first thing they did was restore the name—Marne. It would be called Castle Marne.

On July 17, 2010, the *Denver Post* published an interview with her father, Jim Peiker. "When we bought it in 1988, we knew it was going to be our castle," Peiker said. "And that's how 'Castle Marne' entered circulation."

With his life savings and a Small Business Administration loan, he and Diane, along with daughter Melissa and her husband, Louie, spent the next year refurbishing the historic structure to its former glory. It was literally an upward restoration project. The castle had suffered heavy water damage in the basement due to a burst boiler and pipes. The entire basement contained nearly two feet of standing, rancid water, destroying the hardwood oak floors. The first hurdle at restoration was to repair the basement, secure the foundation and replace the plumbing.

With minimal damage to the exterior structure, the Peiker family next turned their attention to the interior of the mansion. Extensive damage from burst water pipes, most evident in the foyer, had also destroyed the wall along the grand staircase. The wall was repaired and papered in a Victorian red color, popular in the nineteenth century. The once-beautiful staircase was repaired, and hand polishing brought back the original golden oak shine. The "peacock" window had remained intact with very little damage over the past century.

Restoring the interior of the castle to its original state proved to be a daunting task, because of the conversion to apartments by Adele Van Cise in 1918–19. The Peikers' relied on historic photographs found at the Denver Public Library, which allowed them to replicate the interior and many features of the original home. Walls were removed from the apartment era, and the interior was restored as closely as possible to the original 1889 floor plans. While several of the original light fixtures were removed during the conversion to apartments in 1918, the restoration of the mansion was completed with updated electric wiring and included electric fixtures of the original time period.

The ceilings of the main floor were all restored to their original splendor, and the ceiling in the foyer received pressed plaster, returning it to its original design. The walls were covered with replicated wallpaper painted by a restoration painter to represent what was originally in the house. The woodwork throughout the mansion was brought back to its original condition with hand polishing, and repairs included tiger-oak woods. In addition, all of the fireplaces received the same care in returning them to their former glory.

In the formal parlor, to the right of the foyer, once an apartment, a wall was removed, opening the room to its original space. The Peiker family restored the room with vintage furniture, including a large china cabinet against a wall that once had a pull-down bed during the apartment era.

One of the Peikers' employees was a young budding artist named Felix Hopkins. He asked Jim Peiker to allow him to re-create the decorative frieze, a horizontal band near the ceiling, from photographs. Hopkins was able to duplicate the original design, which took him six months to hand paint.

Once an apartment space where Mrs. Adele Van Cise lived until her death, the large dining room was completely restored to its original state. This room includes much of the original Lincrusta wallcovering from England. The beautiful ceiling was painstakingly reproduced, again by Hopkins, with hand-painted flowers around the oval portion and along the top of the walls. An original photo of this ceiling hangs on the wall in the dining room. The reproduction is remarkable. Another interesting aspect to the restoration is evident in this room. Several of the hot-water radiators were either no longer in the home or needed to be replaced. The Peikers' were eventually able to locate replacements from various salvage yards in Denver. While this may seem strange, 1988 was in the era of Denver's Urban Renewal project. Several historic homes were demolished. What to do with disposing such things as radiators? They were sold as scrap to the area's salvage yards.

The second floor was returned to the original four bedrooms and received three additional bathrooms. While one of the bathrooms was being restored, the workers were repairing the marble backsplash above the sink. Removing a piece of the marble tiling, the workers discovered the signature of "Rice & Russell," dated February 1890.

At the end of the hallway is the original master suite, designed for Charles A. Raymond, with a private bathroom and a balcony. The additional three rooms on this floor were also restored to the original floor plan.

The third floor, which once contained the magnificent ballroom, was converted into four guest rooms and four bathrooms. During the restoration of this floor, it was discovered that one of the original fireplaces in the ballroom was gone. It was believed to have been stolen during the time the castle sat vacant. The Peikers' were eventually able to find and purchase a fireplace in an effort to restore the castle as much as possible to its 1889 origin. Jim Peiker located the replacement fireplace in the nearby Clarkco Hotel, which was in the process of being torn down.

Evidence of their acute attention to historical accuracy is evident in the replacement of this fireplace. While the historically accurate fireplace fit the

The dining room includes much of the original Lincrusta wallcovering from England. *Castle Marne.*

space in width, it was shorter than the original, thus leaving the lava stone above exposed. After careful consideration, the Peikers' chose to leave the stone as it was, a relic to the origin of the home. The sweeping oak turn-round of the staircase remains in its original historic glory.

Also on this floor, eight handsome cases display examples of moths and butterflies discovered by John T. Mason, the third owner of Castle Marne. The collection cases were built to the museum staff's specifications by Peiker's son-in-law, Louie Feher-Peiker. The staff of the Museum of Natural Science, which houses John T. Mason's extraordinary collection, then filled them with moths and butterflies displayed today as a memorial to Mr. John T. Mason's scientific research.

The original door, which faces Sixteenth Street, gaining entrance to the original owner's office in the lower level of the home, remains complete with the century-old overhead stone carvings. The carriage mounting step and two of the original hitching posts remain on the Race Street side.

Today

It was a historic event in many aspects when the Castle Marne Bed and Breakfast opened to the public. Opening day was on August 1, 1989, exactly one year to the very day that the Peiker family purchased the property. It was also the 100th anniversary of the construction of the mansion. In addition, the Denver chapter of the American Institute of American Architects, of which Lang, who designed the home, was an 1892 charter member, declared, "The Castle Marne is truly one of Denver's great architectural legacies."

The serendipity continued for the Peiker family, as well as the historic legacy of Castle Marne. Some ten years after the Peiker family purchased Castle Marne, a gentleman by the name of Lee Reedy asked Jim Peiker if he would be interested in purchasing the original 1889 carriage house that sat at the back of his Castle Marne property. Without hesitation, Peiker said, "Yes!" With Peiker's purchase of Raymond's original carriage house, the Castle Marne property was finally restored to its true historic Victorian splendor.

Today, the Castle Marne Bed and Breakfast, one of Denver's finest, provides Victorian lodging, be it overnights, weekend stays or vacation getaways. Personalized accommodations and service are a hallmark of the Peiker family operation. Each of the nine guest rooms are unique, with carefully chosen period furnishings, many of which are from the Peikers' family collection. The charm of Victorian days gone by exudes throughout the castle, lending to a historic, yet comfortable, setting.

A particular delight are the "Traditional Teas." Castle Marne serves traditional afternoon tea, in full Victorian formality, twice daily. Romantic candlelight dinners, held in the formal dining room, are another feature offered to the guests. The dining room also hosts a gourmet breakfast served daily.

Members of the Peiker family are very active in promoting Denver's historic past, serving on many neighborhood boards and committees. They sponsor an annual walking tour of the Wyman Historic District, which ends with a garden party held on the grounds of Castle Marne, one of the most unique architectural designs in the district, created by William Lang.

In fact, during the historical research of the castle and while obtaining photographs from the Denver Public Library, Jim Peiker stumbled on a photo of Colonel James H. Platt's 1894 Denver Paper Mills Company. It was a historic revelation when ties to the Peiker family were discovered.

Contemporary Castle Marne exterior. *Castle Marne.*

During World War I, Platt's former paper mill served as a government facility that produced mustard gas. Following the war, the Continental Label Litho and Folding Box Company purchased the facility.

Peiker's father, Edwin William, was a veteran of the First World War. Peiker served with the Marine Corps in France, as a motorcycle courier for General "Black Jack" Pershing's staff, carrying messages to and from the frontlines to Pershing's headquarters.

Following the war, Peiker returned to Denver in 1918, where he started his own wagon delivery service, working out of a livery stable in a portion of the 1889 Denver City Cable Railway Company building on the corner of Eighteenth and Lawrence Streets in downtown Denver.

One of his customers was the Continental Label Litho and Folding Box Company at Eighteenth and Blake Streets. Peiker was offered a job with the company as a shipping clerk. He accepted the position and soon met and later married Helen Flo Sullivan, who worked at the front desk at the box company. In time, Peiker rose to become the general manager of the company.

Eventually, the owners of the company wanted to sell. Peiker, along with his brothers, Albin and Walter, attempted to buy the company. The newly formed company became known as the Continental Paper Products Company. The employees received small wages yet were also rewarded with shares in the company. In 1926, the company moved out of downtown Denver, relocating in south Denver. The building chosen for business operations was none other than the Denver Paper Mills Company building, constructed in 1890 by Colonel James H. Platt, the second owner of Castle Marne.

As the years went on, the company went through several changes and a few mergers, one of which was the business partnership between Edwin W. Peiker and Walter Paepcke, a wealthy Aspen industrialist. This new company, Central Fiber Products, remained a strong economic force in Denver. Among the many customers was the prestigious Denver department store May D&F. Edwin W. Peiker's company supplied the suit and dress boxes for the department store. The company expanded to supply boxes and bushel baskets for fruit to suppliers across the western United States.

As a high school kid, Jim Peiker worked for the company his father had helped build in the original plant constructed by Colonel Platt. He continued his employment during his college years, moving into a sales position.

And thus, the history of Castle Marne has come full circle.

Today, Castle Marne is a grand showplace open to the public and epitomizing the history of Denver's Victorian era. Jim Peiker said it best in an interview with the *Denver Post* published on July 17, 2010, in which he said, "A Lang house comes with quite a cachet. He lavished carvings on his buildings as grace notes. He's not the only architect who worked here, but many of his finest works are in this neighborhood."

The Peiker family, through their historic preservation efforts, have furthered the legacy of Colorado's Victorian past by offering a glamorous piece of its splendor to the public.

Fun Facts

- One of the two original hitching posts still stands on the Race Street side of the property.
- One of Lang's commercial buildings, known as the Ghost Building, part of the Ghost Block, was later dismantled, stone by stone, in 1980 and stored for a decade. In 1990, the building was laboriously reconstructed at Nineteenth and Stout Streets.
- Castle Marne displays the only sculpted bust of the mansion's architect, William Lang.

- The colonel's widow, Sarah Platt, continued her social work and became known nationally in the women's suffrage movement, working on a national level for equal rights for women. Three times a widow, she overcame personal grief to continue her humanitarian causes. Sarah Platt Decker died in San Francisco, California, in 1912, while attending a conference for the national Federation of Associated Women's Clubs.

- As a result of John T. Mason's butterfly and moth collection, eight species of butterflies are named in his honor. The Mason Hall at the Denver Museum of Natural Science was torn down in 1986 to eventually make way for the Imax building. The John T. Mason collection has been in storage ever since.

- The auction of the Isabella jewels, once owned by Elizabeth "Baby Doe" Tabor and bought by John T. Mason, was conducted by John W. Springer, a Denver banker and horse rancher who owned the Castle Isabel south of Denver.

- The famed Isabella jewels given as a wedding present to Mrs. John T. Mason were eventually sold, save one: a nine-carat pure white diamond. No one knows what became of the incredible diamond. Legend has it that it is somewhere in the Castle Marne. Jim Peiker, owner of the Marne, says that through all the restoration, the house has never revealed the hidden diamond.

- During the restoration process, a framed sepia sketch was found. When owner Jim Peiker took the sketch out of the frame, he discovered printing on the back indicating it belonged to Adele Van Cise. The historic framed sketch is occasionally displayed at Castle Marne.

- In the foyer of Castle Marne, a Carrara marble plant stand is prominently displayed. It was a wedding gift to Edwin and Adele Van Cise. It was returned to the castle as the Peiker family was restoring the building.

- Not long after the Peiker family purchased the historic Denver property, Jim Peiker wanted the beautiful "peacock window" inspected by a professional. He enlisted the services of Watkins Stained Glass Studios of Littleton. The family owned company was begun in 1868 by Watkins's grandfather, Frank Watkins. Philip Watkins Jr. inspected the historic window at Castle Marne. He told Peiker the window was created with Belgium glass and explained the intricate details of the window's construction. After further examination of the window, Watkins told Peiker in a very confident voice, "My grandfather built that window."

- Fortunately, during the restoration of Castle Marne in 1989, Jim Peiker discovered one piece of the historic wood fretwork still present in the home.

It is a two- by three-foot section of interlocking spiral molding under the peacock window on the second-floor landing of the fabulous staircase.

- Over the years, there have been reports of ghosts at Castle Marne. Even various members of the Peiker family have had experiences with ghostly apparitions. Melissa Feher-Peiker says of the ghostly presences, "They give a sense of personality. We coexist and work together."
- In 2010, the city of Denver opened the Van Cise–Simonet Detention Center. The $158 million facility is named after Philip Van Cise, the district attorney who prosecuted criminals, political officials and members of the Ku Klux Klan in the 1920s. He was the son of Adele Van Cise, who owned Castle Marne for nearly twenty years and was responsible for turning the historic edifice into apartments.
- The Raymond House/Castle Marne was placed on the National Register on November 21, 1974, 5DV.123.

Contact Information

CASTLE MARNE BED AND BREAKFAST
1572 Race Street
Denver, Colorado 80206
www.castlemarne.com
(303) 331-0621 or (877) 447-0949

Chapter 6

CASTLE ISABEL—DOUGLAS COUNTY—1891

A PRAIRIE REFUGE

The Beginning

With the establishment of the Colorado Territory in 1861, seventeen counties were created, including Douglas County. This county has the historic distinction of building the first Territorial Road, enacted by the Colorado Territorial Legislature in 1861. This road ran south from Denver City to the settlement of Pueblo. Along the way, the road angled eastward, passing through the valley of Big Dry Creek, then crossed over Plum Creek Divide (near today's Daniels Park.)

This first Territorial Road was instrumental in bringing settlers to the area. Big Dry Creek was one example. Rufus H. "Potato" Clark lived in that area. He found the fertile land conducive to his plan of a potato farm and filed a homestead claim in 1859. Experimenting that first year, his initial harvest was so successful that the following year he planted his entire acreage in potatoes. So abundant were Clark's potato fields that he was not only selling his crop locally, but he was also hauling the produce north to the Denver market.

Other homesteaders, ranchers and farmers began to settle in the Big Dry Creek area. Perhaps the most notable farmer of the era was Johanne Welte, an Austrian immigrant who came to the area in 1878. Welte, along with his brother-in-law Plazidus Gasner, purchased 160 acres of land along Big Dry Creek. The semiarid land was suitable for dry farming, which was exactly what the two men intended to do. However, the men had spent all the money they had on the land. Eventually, they were able to secure a loan, at 18 percent interest, to buy twenty dairy cows. It took time, but with hard work, they improved their dairy operation, which they named the Big Dry Creek Cheese Ranch.

The cheese operation, which the locals fondly referred to as the Welte Cheese Ranch, produced the finest qualities of milk, butter, Brick and Limburger cheeses known not only in Douglas County but across the state as well.

By 1890, wealthy businessmen and ranchers began buying land in the area. Samuel Allen Long was one of these men. Long, a native of Pennsylvania, filed for a forty-acre homestead on land next to Welte's cheese farm in 1884. Why he chose to file a homestead claim is unclear as Long was a very wealthy man, having made his fortune through Pennsylvania's mighty railroad industry. Nevertheless, he began a profitable ranching enterprise.

In 1891, Long began construction of his new home on the prairie. It was a large home, built of local stone quarried in nearby Castle Rock. He named it Rotherwood, the same name as the Pennsylvania family farm where he grew up. Over the next few years, Long bought several homesteads, eventually increasing his landholdings to two thousand acres.

Well-respected Texas cattleman John Wallace Springer, who had recently moved to Denver, soon learned of the open space and quality of land in Douglas County. He slowly and quietly began buying land, eventually becoming another neighbor of Welte's.

Springer, an Illinois native, practiced law in that state for ten years before moving west. He settled in Texas, where in June 1891, he married Eliza Clifton Hughes, the daughter of a wealthy cattleman in the Dallas area, Colonel William E. Hughes. Springer handled the financial interests of his father-in-law's ranching enterprise and eventually became an influential member of the Texas cattle industry in his own right. Meanwhile, Eliza gave birth to two daughters, Annie Clifton and Sarah Elizabeth. Sadly, Sarah died in the first year of her life.

In 1897, in an effort to relieve Eliza's severe tuberculosis, Springer relocated his family to the Denver area. With his background as an attorney and through his various enterprises, Springer became a prominent Denver businessman. He served as the first president of the National Cattlemen's Association, established in 1898, a position he held for eight consecutive years and, at the same time, became the director of Denver's Capitol National Bank. Springer ran for mayor of Denver against Robert Speer in the election of 1904 but was defeated.

John W. Springer built Springer Ranch and renamed it Castle Isabel for his second wife. *Denver Public Library.*

Glory Days

Through his successful land purchases, within a year Springer had acquired several thousand acres in Douglas County. Two of his purchases included the original 160-acre homestead claim of Mary Burkhardt and Samuel A. Long's acres located next to Welte's cheese farm. It was on Long's original homestead land, which already had several buildings, that Springer began the development of a pedigree horse ranch.

In 1901, Springer's father-in-law, the wealthy Colonel Hughes, joined in the horse operation. Together the two increased the ranch size to twenty-three thousand acres. The two men purchased three award-winning Oldenburg stallions and 150 quality mares. These extraordinary animals were imported from Germany, where their blood pedigree went back several centuries. The Springer Cross Country Horse and Cattle Ranch soon gained a reputation for the quality of its horses. Springer stated in his business model, "The avowed purpose of the ranch is to turn out an ideal American Coach horse, with sense, style, action, substance, and endurance." With such a successful beginning, Springer began the expansion of his ranch by improving the buildings on the land and erecting new ones, including large horse barns to house the increasing number of horses. The original brick silos connected to the barns on the property provided storage for cattle feed during the winter. A windmill was erected high on a hill on the southern portion of the land and operated the primary well providing water for the ranch.

At the same time, Springer began the construction of his stately mansion. In an unusual step for a man of such wealth, rather than start anew, Springer chose to work with what he already had. He remodeled and expanded Long's original stone house into a German baron-style mansion. Complementing the structure, lavender and pink rhyolite stone quarried in Castle Rock was used for both the exterior and interior walls. Ironstone was used for the many improvements and additions to the remaining original structures.

The renovation and expansion of the stone house progressed into the eventual mansion Springer had envisioned and continued into the spring of 1904. However, tragedy struck the John Springer family. His beloved wife, Eliza, died on May 22 of that year from her illness. Following the death of his wife, a bereaved Springer remained in seclusion with his daughter, Annie, at the Denver residence at 930 Washington Street, a home he had purchased just the previous year.

Castle Isabel, later named for John Springer's second wife, was completed in 1891. *Douglas County Historical Society.*

When the mansion was completed later that year, it was a grand structure. The two-story stone edifice, constructed of massive rhyolite stone walls over three feet thick, included a four-story tower at one corner, which served as the entrance to the Springer home, giving the stately mansion a feel of feudal splendor. Beautiful stone pillars supported the iron fencing at the front. A private courtyard graced the rear of the grounds.

Inside, the stone walls were enhanced with high-rising stucco and timbered ceilings. The main floor included a formal receiving room, a large dining room, a kitchen complete with a butler's pantry, a billiard room, a library and a grand ballroom. The floor of the ballroom was polished oak, which was covered by Navajo rugs for protection when not in use. The rooms of the main floor were decorated with a western flair, including draperies made of doeskin, and the furniture was often adorned with deer antlers. An elegant staircase led to the bedrooms for the family and quarters for the staff, which encompassed the second story of the mansion.

Quite pleased with his mansion, Springer called it Springer's Castle. In time, he returned to the ranching enterprise, although still suffering under a cloud of misery and loneliness. The Cross Country Horse and Cattle Ranch became one of the top ranches in the state and home to prizewinning show horses both locally and nationally. Under Springer's effective management, his stock gained attention and respect around the world. A local Douglas County advertisement read in part, "offering a uniformity in the Oldenburg breed as to appearance, color and gait, and high knee action that at once stamped him as being extraordinary."

And the Rest Is History

In early 1906, the somewhat reclusive John Springer began to venture out in social settings. As the widower was searching for a brighter light, he met the irresistible Isabel Patterson Folck. The young woman was staying in Denver during one of her many trips. During the summer of 1906, she returned to Denver, and the two soon began a more-than-cordial relationship. As the relationship intensified, Springer would later testify, "I was smitten." By the end of summer, Isabel returned to St. Louis, where she eventually obtained a divorce so that she could marry the wealthy widower.

Meanwhile, even before the marriage, Colonel Hughes, Springer's father-in-law, disapproved of the relationship. As whispers of indiscretion and promiscuity on the part of Mrs. Isabel Patterson Folck increased in Denver circles, the colonel obtained legal custody of his granddaughter, Springer's only living child, Annie.

Isabel Patterson grew up in the suburbs of St. Louis, Missouri, where she was known as a social butterfly. She soon married John E. Folck, a traveling shoe salesman. However, the marriage did not hold the interest of the young freewheeling Isabel. She began to travel alone, and it was during one of her trips that she met the lonely yet quite wealthy and prominent widower John Wallace Springer.

Springer was indeed smitten, and the wedding took place in St. Louis three weeks after Isabel obtained the divorce in April 1907. In a lavish ceremony, the forty-seven-year-old Springer took the former Mrs. Isabel Patterson Folck as his bride. She was twenty-seven years old.

Following the St. Louis wedding, the couple returned to Colorado, first setting up housekeeping at Springer's Denver home. The Springers also spent considerable time at the horse ranch, where they lived in seemingly happy matrimony—for a time, at least. Springer even renamed his mansion "Castle Isabel" in honor of his bride. As Springer went back to the management of his ranch and his beloved horses, it wasn't long before Isabel became bored and yearned for the night life she left behind when she became Mrs. John W. Springer. Evidently, Springer didn't mind, as he rented a suite at the Brown Palace Hotel in downtown Denver, where she could stay after late-night parties with friends. It would be the beginning of unforeseen marital problems for Springer, and marital problems would also plague future owners of the mansion.

Whether Springer was too busy with his considerable business affairs or he simply turned a blind eye to the actions of his new bride, his former

Isabel Patterson Springer became the center of a triangular love tryst that resulted in murder and Denver's most sensational murder trial. *Denver Public Library.*

father-in-law and business partner, Colonel Hughes, did take notice and action. In 1909, Hughes sold his interests in every company associated with his former son-in-law.

During one of her many independent travels to St. Louis to visit friends, Isabel met an adventurous thirty-two-year-old entrepreneur and avid balloonist, Sylvester Louis "Tony" Von Phul. He and Isabel began an intimate relationship that would be an on-again, off-again affair Isabel would continue for the next few years. Meanwhile, in March 1911, during a visit to her husband's office in downtown Denver, Isabel met a client of her husband's, Mr. Harold Francis (Frank) Henwood, an adventurous businessman in his own right. The Springers enjoyed Henwood's company and often invited him to their home and to social events. It wasn't long before Henwood began spending considerable time—including overnight stays—at the Springer ranch when Mr. Springer was out of town on business. In the midst of this affair, Isabel rekindled the relationship with Von Phul through a series of love letters.

As Isabel's letters to Von Phul escalated into a feverish tone in May 1911, Henwood discovered evidence of Isabel's other love interest. In a heated confrontation, Isabel tearfully confessed to the trysts yet insisted the relationship was over. She told Henwood that Von Phul had several "silly" love letters she had written and was threatening to send the letters to her husband. She asked Henwood to help her stop Von Phul from revealing the affair to her husband, to which he readily agreed. Then, in a strange twist of events, Isabel wrote to Von Phul in a letter dated May 20, 1911, insisting he come to Denver immediately and meet her at the Brown Palace Hotel.

The true intentions of Isabel Patterson Springer can never be known, for her testimony at the subsequent murder trial revealed nothing but denials and self-perceived innocence. In any case, on the night of May 24, 1911, Isabel's two paramours met face to face at the prestigious Marble Bar inside the Brown Palace Hotel. The two men exchanged words and then threw punches. Then gunshots rang out. As the pandemonium in the bar subsided, Von Phul and an innocent bystander lay on the floor, while Henwood stood nearby with a gun in his hand. Among the many witnesses to the shooting were Mr. and Mrs. John W. Springer.

The June 5, 1911 issue of the *Denver Post* printed an article with the headline "VON PHUL SHOT IN ROW OVER MRS. SPRINGER, FRIENDS SAY."

The article went on to detail the love triangle between the accused murderer, the victim and "the woman." The reporter also mentioned eight "love" letters found in Von Phul's hotel room, concluding, "Mrs. Springer enjoyed the most friendly relations with Von Phul." The article not only named Mrs. Isabel Springer but also featured her photo.

This was the first of many newspaper stories over the next several months covering Denver's sensational murder trial. But it was enough for John W. Springer. The day after the article appeared, he filed for divorce from Isabel, "the woman" sensationalized by being in the center of Denver's salacious murder and for whom he had so lovingly renamed his mansion.

As the murder trial dragged on, with both Springers testifying, the experience took an emotional toll on John Springer. During this time, the divorce between

John W. Springer and his wife, Isabel Patterson Springer, enter the courthouse during the murder trial of her lover, Sylvester Louis "Tony" Von Phul. *Denver Public Library.*

Mr. and Mrs. Springer had been finalized. As part of the divorce settlement, the ex-Mrs. Springer was to leave Denver and never return. After the trial ended, Isabel left town on the very next eastbound train.

In 1913, Springer transferred the deed of his land and the mansion to his former father-in-law, Colonel Hughes, who continued the legacy of the venerable horse ranch Springer had envisioned. However, his first act was to rename the property and the mansion. He called it the "Sunland Ranch." He made improvements to the interior of the mansion and added furniture and art to suit his tastes. A few of his favorite pieces were a set of cowhide leather chairs and a matching love seat. They were made of horns from Texas longhorn cattle, and the leather was dyed a purple shade. Another favorite piece was a tall solid black walnut hutch that also served as a buffet center. It stood elegantly along one wall of the dining room. Along another wall of this room was a long shelf where the colonel proudly displayed his collection of German beer steins. Other interior improvements included combining the library and billiard room into one large recreation room. This room contained a pool table at one end and a large reading table at the other end, with several large bookshelves.

When Colonel Hughes died in 1918, Springer's daughter, Annie, inherited the property. Annie Clifton Springer had married Lafayette Hughes (no relation to her grandfather) the previous year. During the two years that Annie and her husband owned the property, very few changes were made.

In 1920, Annie and her husband sold the mansion and the ranch property to Waite Phillips, the brother of Phillips Petroleum founders Frank and Lee E. Phillips of Oklahoma. Phillips renamed the property "Highland Ranch" for the Highland Hereford breed of cattle he raised on the ranch. After six years, in 1926, he sold the property and the mansion to Frank E. Kistler for $425,000.

Kistler, the president of Wolhurst Farms, had big plans for the ranch. He renamed the property the "Diamond K Ranch," establishing a new ranching enterprise. No longer known for prized horses, the historic ranch, under Kistler's ownership, focused on raising Angus cattle, dairy cattle, purebred sheep, hogs and chickens. The dairy operation included the milking barns, hay barns and a bunkhouse for the many ranch hands who worked for Kistler.

As the cattle business began to improve and show a favorable profit, Kistler and his wife, Florence, began extensive renovations and additions to the mansion. To achieve the classic style of English Tudor Revival architecture that the couple desired, Kistler hired Denver architect Jules Jacques Benois Benedict. Benedict's work was quite visible in the Denver area, including the Boat House at Washington Park, the home of the Coors family in Golden, Littleton's First Presbyterian Church, the Holy Ghost Church in Denver and Denver's Gart Brothers' building on Broadway.

Benedict added a west wing in the desired English Tudor style to the exterior of the mansion, complemented with a high gabled shake-shingle roof. The interior of the mansion continued the theme. Nine rooms were added with large fireplaces and hardwood floors. Benedict also added, in accordance with the Kistlers' elaborate desires, a secret panel, two secret passageways and a bowling alley.

The Kistlers eventually divorced in 1929. Not long after the divorce, Frank Kistler married Leana Antonides, the widow of Ralph Antonides, a well-known Denver businessman involved in oil and real estate.

That very year, Kistler took the bold step of inviting the acclaimed Arapahoe Hunt Club to transfer its Denver headquarters at the Denver Country Club to the open prairie land of his Diamond K Ranch. The hunting club, with the encouragement of its president, Lawrence Cowle Phipps Jr., readily agreed to the move. Members of this prestigious hunt club enjoyed the thrill of hunting coyotes on horseback on Kistler's ranch, and Phipps and Kistler became lifelong friends.

Unfortunately, the severe economic turmoil of the Great Depression caused financial difficulties for Kistler. In 1937, he was forced to sell the Diamond K Ranch. Fortunately for Kistler, his good friend Lawrence Phipps Jr. was able to help him out of his financial predicament. After negotiations that included Lawrence Cowle Phipps Sr., the Phipps family purchased the Diamond K Ranch and mansion from Kistler for $250,000.

The Phipps family was well known not only in Colorado but across the nation as well. The family hailed from Pennsylvania, where the senior Phipps rose through the ranks to eventually become the first vice-president of the powerful Carnegie Steel Company of that state. In 1901, Phipps moved his family to Colorado, where he immediately became involved in local business and politics. However, gossip floated through the circles of the social elite when Phipps married for the third time in 1911. His bride was Miss Margaret Rogers, the daughter of Platt Rogers, wealthy attorney and Denver's former mayor. The social tongues wagged, as the bride was twenty-six years younger than the groom. The winds of gossip must have eventually died down, for Phipps ran for and won election in 1918 to the United States Senate from the state of Colorado.

With the purchase of the ranch, the Phipps family continued the ranching operations, yet with a heavier focus on the cattle. While the Phipps family held the controlling interest in the property, it was Lawrence Phipps Jr., an army veteran, having served during World War I, who managed the cattle ranch, which he renamed "Highlands Ranch." Whether the name change was simply reverting to Phipps's original name in honor of the successful cattle breed or for the high bluffs and sweeping hills along the prairie is pure speculation.

For the next forty years, Lawrence Phipps Jr. and various members of his family lived in the mansion. One such member who had limited involvement was his brother Allan R. Phipps. A Denver attorney, Allan often handled legal matters pertaining to the ranch. During those years, Phipps Jr. sold off some of the original landholdings and acquired additional land. In 1943, he purchased the neighboring Welte Cheese Farm on Big Dry Creek. With this land purchase, the Phipps' Highlands Ranch property encompassed twenty-two thousand acres, reaching southeast to join the land of Douglas County's venerable Charlford Ranch. Phipps also continued the long-standing tradition of the Arapahoe Hunt Club. The Highlands Ranch remained the headquarters of the prestigious riding club for nearly four decades.

Lawrence Phipps Jr. and his wife, the former Bertha Richmond, experienced marital problems, as had previous owners of the mansion. Phipps and his first wife, Gladys Hart Phipps, had divorced in 1930 after eighteen years of marriage.

Shortly after his divorce, he married Miss Richmond. In 1938, just one year after the couple had moved into the Highlands Ranch mansion, they divorced. In 1945, Phipps married for a third time, this time to a talented Denver artist by the name of Elaine Oaks. The couple lived happily in the mansion and worked together in making improvements to the ranching operations.

In 1964, Phipps's brothers, Allan and Gerald, bought the Denver Broncos franchise. Under their ownership, they put together a winning team, increased sales and profits and were instrumental in building the Mile High Stadium. The Phipps family owned the Broncos franchise for the next seventeen years.

In 1976, Lawrence Phipps Jr. died following a long illness. After his death, the entire estate, including the various business investments, the Highlands Ranch property and mansion, was sold to oil tycoon Marvin Davis, owner of the Davis Oil Corporation, for over $13 million.

Davis had no interest in the mansion or the historic value of the property. He immediately formed the Highlands Ventures Corporation in an effort to market the land for subdivision into residential homes. In 1978, the California-based development company of Mission Viejo Corporation, a subsidiary of Philip Morris Inc., took out a two-year lease option on the land. The idea of subdivision was so popular that the corporation bought the twenty-two-acre historic property outright the following year.

The Mission Viejo Corporation marketed its model homes beginning in 1980. Fortunately for the historic preservation and historical value of the Highlands Ranch mansion, Phil and Kaye Scott bought the mansion in 1981. Then in 1997, the historic mansion and surrounding ranch land was purchased by the real estate firm of Shea Homes, which held the title for thirteen years. While the mansion remained virtually intact, most of the land was sold for urban development. In 2002, a group of citizens working to save the historic Highlands Ranch mansion were successful in placing a bond issue on the county voter ballot that would have funded the purchase of the mansion. Unfortunately, the voters of the Highlands Ranch community defeated the bond measure.

Today

In April 2010, Shea Homes conveyed the ownership to the Highlands Ranch Metro District, along with a $4 million endowment for restoration and operating expenses.

Restoration of the neglected mansion began in the summer of 2010. Rick Owens, chairman of the board of the metro district, said, "This is going to be the place for us to gather to learn about our heritage, to learn about the Front Range, all of Douglas County."

During the next two years, extensive renovation of the mansion included a new roof, a new heating system, air conditioning and a complete overhaul of the plumbing systems. A common theme among the different owners was that each one made many changes. "What was fortunate was that the building was in pretty good shape for as old as it is," said Terry Nolan, general manager for the Highlands Ranch Metro District. Jeff Case, the director of public works for the metro district and project manager for the renovations, echoed Nolan's statements, saying, "They added wings, added rooms, and they took things down and put things back." He also revealed that the work was challenging because there were no architectural blueprints to use since the mansion had been changed and altered by the various owners. In that sense, the Highlands Ranch mansion is quite possibly the most unique mansion, in regard to its architectural history, in all of Colorado.

Due to neglect, the mansion had experienced obvious destabilizing over the years. While keeping the historic integrity of the building, a few walls deemed unsafe were torn down, including a decades-old stone wall on the south side. Another wall that couldn't be saved because of rotted wood revealed a historic find. When the wall was torn down, the stone foundation revealed an etched word in the stone: "Rotherwood." This was the name the original builder, Samuel Long, had given his home and property. Whenever possible, salvageable historic pieces of the original building, such as the quarried stone from the demolished south wall, were incorporated into other renovations or new structures on the property. This was the case when the new Carriage House Pavilion was built. The exterior walls of the pavilion were constructed with locally quarried stone to match as closely as possible to the exterior of the mansion and also incorporated the stone from the demolished south wall.

When the renovations were completed, the exterior had received a much-needed facelift but remained true to the historic origins of the structure. Inside the twenty-two-thousand-square-foot mansion, the historic integrity of the previous owners remained. The mansion includes most of the additions from the various owners, including Springer's additions of the ballroom (later referred to as the "great" room), the fabulous wooden staircase, the kitchen and adjoining butler's pantry and the dining room. The remodeling done by Springer's father-in-law is also evident in the library and recreation

Contemporary castle exterior. *Linda Wommack.*

room. The fourteen bedrooms and most of the eleven bathrooms reflect the original Victorian architecture and décor. The Victorian décor is prominent throughout the mansion, although the Art Deco styles of owners Frank Kistler and Waite Phillips are also evident. Several pieces of art, including sculptures and paintings belonging to various owners of the mansion, enhance many rooms.

The Highlands Ranch Mansion opened as an event center in the summer of 2012. Community events are held throughout the year both inside the mansion and on the property. From daily tours of the mansion to elegant weddings, conventions, business conferences and meetings, special events and corporate parties, there is much to see and do.

History blends with the contemporary in a most attractive way. The surrounding 250 acres reflect the lifestyle of the early settlers and pioneers. The cattle and dairy barns, the bunkhouse and the brick silos still remain. The historic windmill—operational after all these years, although now powered by electricity—stands on the south hill as a sentinel over the mansion, as it has for over a century.

The historic mansion stands today not only as a valuable piece of history but also a testament to the many owners of such a grand place who truly held to the Colorado pioneer spirit.

Fun Facts

- Rufus H. "Potato" Clark's original 1859 homestead claim is now the site of the Highlands Ranch Golf Club.
- In December 1907, the estate auction of the Isabella jewels, once owned by Elizabeth "Baby Doe" Tabor, was held on the front steps of the International Trust Bank. The auction was conducted by John W. Springer, a trustee of the bank. The buyer was John T. Mason, owner of Denver's Castle Marne.
- Frank E. Kistler, who called the historic property the "Diamond K Ranch" during his ownership from 1926 to 1937, left his mark in several places of the mansion. One can still see a pattern of diamonds and the embedded "K" in the sandstone fireplace in the main parlor.
- During restoration of the mansion, a construction worker discovered an old postcard addressed to former mansion owner Lawrence Phipps Jr., inviting him to a glee club show in Denver featuring the Whiffenpoofs, a 1950s group that ironically was performing in town in December, the month that the postcard was discovered.
- As the renovation of the mansion progressed in 2010, the Highlands Ranch Historical Society uncovered just one set of blueprints, which is puzzling, given all the additions over the years. Even more puzzling, according to project manager Jeff Case, the one available blueprint wasn't followed. The blueprint was dated at the time period of the stock market crash. Case surmised, "I think it was a kind of grand plan from Frank Kistler and then the market crashed and they just never followed through with it."
- While removing interior walls, construction workers stumbled on doorways and windows and even a secret passageway that had been boarded up by previous owners and unknown to subsequent owners.
- The history of the Highlands Ranch area played a part in James A. Michener's 1974 best-selling novel of Colorado's history, *Centennial*. The pioneer story of Rufus H. "Potato" Clark was portrayed in the character of "Potato Brumbaugh." The Highlands Ranch mansion itself also

received notoriety through Michener's work. In 1978, the televised miniseries *Centennial* featured the exterior of the mansion for the fictional Venneford Ranch. The sign "Venneford Ranch," made for the film, hung over the entrance to the property for several years.

Contact Information

THE HIGHLANDS RANCH MANSION
9900 South Ranch Road
Highlands Ranch, Colorado 80126
www.highlandsranch.com.
(720) 542-8392

Chapter 7

GABLE HOUSE—DURANGO—1892

DURANGO'S VICTORIAN DIAMOND

The Silvery San Juans. With the wealth of silver discoveries in Colorado's southern mountain range and the booming railroad industry in full force a decade following the Civil War, it wasn't a matter of *if* the railroads could cross the mountain range. Instead, it was a matter of when and which railroad would first succeed.

The Beginning

Former Civil War general William Jackson Palmer and his right-hand man, Dr. William A. Bell, had successfully built their Denver & Rio Grande railroad enterprise through the area of the Royal Gorge canyon, constructing the hanging bridge, a marvel that survives to this day. By using the newest technology—narrow-gauge rails—Palmer was able to beat his competitors to the San Juan area, with a new line from Alamosa to Durango. Surveying and good intelligence revealed that the curving valley of the Animas River was low enough, by several thousand feet, and nearer to the silver mines of Silverton than any other route and thus was the best course for the railroad. The valley also held other resources advantageous to the railroad: an abundance of coal reserves, water and a fine spot for a railroad town and future expansion in all directions. Railroad construction began in 1879.

As vice-president of the Denver & Rio Grande Railroad, Dr. Bell arrived in the Animas River Valley, surrounded by the San Juan Mountains, during the rail construction to promote the railroad and lay out a town site. The town of Animas City had high aspirations of becoming the rail center for the San Juan area. The powerful Denver & Rio Grande Railroad, in negotiations, asked for certain land rights and other concessions in return for a nearly guaranteed economic boom to the city. So sure that Animas City was the only choice available to the railroad company, the city fathers brazenly refused all offers and concessions. Dr. Bell urged reconsideration, or the railroad would be forced to find land and build the town of its vision elsewhere. Unfortunately for Animas City, they were firm in their own demands. Undaunted, Dr. Bell, in his surveys, found excellent flat land some two miles south of Animas City, yet still along the river, as water was an obvious necessity.

On September 13, 1880, the railroad town of Durango came into being. General Palmer, along with his transportation enterprise, was also a town promoter. He would become known throughout the state for developing communities along his railroad lines, the first being Colorado Springs. He perfected that idea with Durango, where his careful planning is evident throughout the town to this day.

Palmer set up a town company, known as the Durango Trust, which included such prominent businessmen as Alexander C. Hunt, the former territorial governor. This group was entrusted with planning the long-term future of Durango. The first plat of the town, dated September 1880, shows a grand boulevard with designations for churches and residential communities. The trust company donated lots for the first church, the first school and the lot for the city hall building. The "main" street was the street of commerce and commercial enterprise.

Even before the railroad arrived, Palmer and the Durango Trust built an ore smelter at the outskirts of the town and developed the nearby coal region for mining. Palmer instinctively knew all of these assets would bring growth to his railroad town, as well as business for his railroad.

The *Durango Herald*, which published its first paper on June 23, 1881, followed with a local blockbuster story in its July 28, 1881 issue:

The iron horse arrived in Durango about five o'clock yesterday afternoon. A large crowd gathered soon after at the corner of G and Railroad streets to witness the driving of the silver spike. With a well directed blow by Mayor Taylor, the silver spike was driven home. "This symbolizes the completion of the city and the Rio Grande brings enterprise and prosperity for all." The silver used in the spike came from the well-known mines up Junction Creek, and is of the best quality.

By September, sales of town lots skyrocketed, even at inflated prices. Durango's first Christmas was celebrated by over two thousand residents of the new city. The following spring, according to the *Durango Record*, among the businesses along Main Avenue were five lumber companies, four hardware stores, three mercantile establishments, twenty saloons and ten real estate firms.

Durango's proximity to the lucrative coal mines provided not only employment for many citizens of Durango but also the needed fuel for businesses and home heating. It was the local coal mining companies that provided the needed power for generating electricity, which, in 1887, made Durango one of the first cities in Colorado to go electric. The energy created by electricity was a boom to the development of the young town, as the January 12, 1888 issue of the *Durango Herald* reflected, writing, "The electric light is becoming popular and should be used in every business house and residence in the city."

Durango's economy not only grew but also thrived, just as General Palmer predicted. Two of those early businessmen, both owners of two of the original mercantile establishments, would figure intimately in the history of Durango's Gable House.

Glory Days

James Schutt was a wealthy businessman by the time he built his grand home in 1892. Much of his wealth came from real estate dealings in Durango and the Four Corners area. When the town of Durango was created, Schutt established one of the first of the three mercantile stores, as well as a flour mill. With his success, Schutt built a home at 805 Fifth Avenue for himself and his wife, Eliza.

The Victorian mansion was designed and built by George S. Barber. Built in the popular Queen Anne style of the era, the three-story home was a prominent structure in the new residential area. Constructed of deep-red brick, kilned in Pueblo, the exterior of the home featured a wooden wraparound porch with ornate banisters. Two decorative balconies enhanced the second floor. A fabulous turret crowned the corner of the third floor. There were four gables, which joined the steeply pitched main roof, each of which featured fish-scaled shingles with ornate fascia at the gable ends.

The interior of the home featured a formal parlor and dining room on the first floor, with bedrooms on the second floor. Hardwood floors, made of oak, graced the mansion.

James and Eliza Schutt, who never had children, enjoyed their home for the next few years, despite the economic disaster of the repeal of the Sherman Silver Purchase Act in 1893. It is quite possible that Schutt felt an economic downturn was in the making, as he had signed over the deed to the mansion to his wife, Eliza, prior to the silver crash. It is also most likely the reason the third floor of the home was never finished during their ownership.

Following the repeal, Durango, along with most of Colorado, fell into an economic depression. As mines closed overnight, the effect rippled across the state. In Durango, fifteen businesses failed by early summer. Palmer's Rio Grande Southern Railroad fell into receivership. By the end of the summer, there were three workers for every two jobs available.

The Schutt Mercantile remained open, although sales were dismal. By Christmas, retailers, including Schutt, were advertising discounts, offering a "deep cut on holiday goods." His competitor, J.L. Rachofsky, who owned the Famous, another mercantile, advertised the previous year's inventory for sale "at cost."

While Schutt's various businesses suffered through what came to be known as the worst depression of the century, he and Eliza eventually liquidated many of their holdings, including their home. In 1898, the mansion was sold, ironically enough, to J.L. Rachofsky, Schutt's mercantile competitor.

The Famous lived up to its name, selling everything from beans and flour to hammers and nails, as well as clothing, shoes and boots. While it was not the only mercantile in town, it was the most "famous" for catering to the common working family.

Tragedy occurred in 1913, when fire engulfed the Famous, destroying Rachofsky's business. Financially ruined, Rachofsky sold the mansion to its most illustrious owner.

And the Rest Is History

Dr. Benjamin J. Ochsner was renowned as one of the finest physicians in southwestern Colorado. He left his medical practice in Telluride, moving to Durango, where he practiced at Durango's Mercy Hospital. After a disagreement with the hospital board of practitioners over a variety of issues regarding medical practice, Dr. Ochsner purchased the mansion from Rachofsky for the sole purpose of running his own hospital.

Dr. Ochsner oversaw an extensive conversion of the home. The first-floor rooms were opened to create a larger area, which Ochsner used as a patient ward for needy patients. The former parlor was used as Ochsner's private office. The second-floor rooms were private patient rooms, with a few two-bed rooms. The third floor, which had never been completed by either of the previous owners, was transformed into the operating room. The glass in the windows was replaced with leaded prismatic glass tiles, which actually diffused the sunlight coming into room, eliminating any reflection on the operating table. Dr. Ochsner purchased a "carriage house" of sorts and had it moved to the back of the property. This was used as a residence for his nurses.

The Ochsner Hospital, which opened in 1913, became Durango's first private hospital. Ochsner and his hospital served the community quite admirably. Lives were saved by Dr. Ochsner's renowned medical expertise and his surgical skills. Ochsner furthered his practice by installing the first X-ray machine in the county.

Seven years after the hospital was opened, county health regulations required Ochsner to install linoleum flooring, as it was easier to clean for sanitation purposes. Complying with the new regulation, Ochsner installed the required flooring over the original oak flooring.

Dr. Ochsner was already a wealthy man by the time he opened his hospital. He owned not one but four Pierce Arrow automobiles, which were often the topic of gossip in Durango. He was also known internationally as an award-winning competitor in the sport of pistol shooting. He would practice his shooting skills in the cellar of his home on the corner of Fourth Avenue and Seventh Street, just a block away from his Ochsner Hospital. The good doctor's second claim to international fame was as an award-winning photographer. Ochsner created some of his best artwork in the 1920s and 1930s, using a style of gelatin silver print, as well as carbon print. Ochsner was one of the very few photographers who still developed prints using the outdated carbon process. Ochsner sensitized his printing paper and used natural sunlight to develop his prints. As such, he was considered one of the world's most consistent contributors to both national and international photography venues. Dr. Ochsner was among the few American artists to be honored with a fellowship in the Royal Photography Society of London.

When Dr. Benjamin J. Ochsner retired in 1937, Drs. Leo Lloyd and Christopher Martin purchased the facility. They continued Dr. Ochsner's hospital practice for the next five years. In 1942, the doctors sold the property to La Plata County officials, who operated the hospital as the county's first public hospital, later known as the Community Hospital, for the next twenty years.

In 1962, the county officials deemed the hospital outdated and opened a new facility. The property was then sold to the JAME Corporation. An acronym for four wealthy investors, one of the investors, Marvin Dale, eventually purchased the property outright in 1966. For the next five years, Dale operated the mansion as a rooming house for students attending Durango's Fort Lewis College.

Today

In 1971, Jeffrey and Heather Bryson purchased the historic edifice from Marvin Dale. The Brysons began a lengthy and painstaking restoration process, the ultimate goal being to return the mansion to its original condition. It would take years.

As the Brysons began their restoration process, all the while they continued to operate the mansion as a rooming house to the local college students.

The structure and foundation were found to be in relatively good shape. The Pueblo red brick had proven to be a wise choice for the 1892 building. However, the weatherworn century-old elaborate woodwork along the porch and both balconies was replaced. The interior was an entirely different matter.

Broken windows throughout the house were replaced. Layers and layers of paint were painstakingly stripped from the walls. Through their research, the Brysons were then able to find period-correct paint matches for the walls. The linoleum was torn up from the floors. Sadly, the original oak floors underneath were in bad condition. With hard work, golden oak flooring was eventually refurbished to the original condition.

The entryway to Gable House features the restored original wood floors. *Ben Martinez*.

Known as the music room, this room is quite inviting. *Ben Martinez*.

This formal parlor is a cozy room with eclectic adornments. *Ben Martinez*.

In the charming dining room, a lovely painting hangs on the wall. The youngest of the three girls is now the owner of Gable House. *Ben Martinez*.

Gable House exterior. *Ben Martinez.*

The second and third floors of the mansion had suffered considerable damage from a roof that had apparently been leaking for years. "It was sheer neglect," said Heather Bryson. The water damage affected several walls, floors and the ceilings. The entire roof was replaced. This proved to be quite a daunting task. From the corner turret to the steeply pitched points, attention was paid to historic accuracy. The four gables also received careful consideration in an effort to duplicate the fish-scaled shingles at the gable ends. It may have been serendipity, for the Brysons chose to name their bed-and-breakfast Gable House.

In 1994, the Brysons opened Gable House to the public as a bed-and-breakfast. Today, the Gable House Bed and Breakfast offers not only a true Victorian experience for their guests but a warm and friendly atmosphere as well. Heather Bryson says, "The Gable House is an intimate B&B. You come in contact with me, not a desk clerk. I truly care about my guests and want them only to go away glowing, rested, rejuvenated and telling their friends what a wonderful time they had."

Indeed, the Gable House Bed and Breakfast has flourished under the care and ownership of Heather Bryson. Throughout her years of ownership, Heather Bryson has paid careful attention to the mansion's architectural features and historic importance in the community of Durango. As a result of her hard work and attention to historic detail, the 1892 home was placed on the National Register of Historic Places in 1995 and was featured in the May issue of the *Victorian Homes Sourcebook* the same year.

James Schutt would surely be pleased with the Victorian splendor that is Durango's Gable House Bed and Breakfast.

Fun Facts

- A few of Doctor Ochsner's award-winning photographs are housed at the Smithsonian Institute. Durango's Fort Lewis College also holds a collection of some four hundred photographs of Ochsner's work.
- Heather Bryson, owner of Gable House, says, "In my forty years of being in the house, I have not experienced any spirits." However, she did go on to say, "Years ago, I had, at three separate times, Native American students tell me they saw a spirit."
- Gable House, (Ochsner Hospital) was placed on the National Register May 4, 1995, 5LP.1336.

Contact Information

GABLE HOUSE BED AND BREAKFAST
805 Fifth Avenue
Durango, Colorado 81301
www.durangobedandbreakfast.com
(970) 247-4982

Chapter 8

ROSEMOUNT—PUEBLO—1893

THE ROSE OF PUEBLO

The Beginning

The Thatcher brothers were Colorado pioneers, merchandisers by trade, during the gold rush days, millionaires by the turn of the century. Often overlooked in the pages of history, the story of the Thatcher brothers is an epic account of Colorado frontier success.

Twenty-three-year-old John Albert Thatcher, the eldest of three brothers, ventured west for success and fortune. His intention wasn't for the gold in the hills but rather the fabulous business opportunities Denver City had to offer.

Arriving in Denver City on September 15, 1862, Thatcher was dismayed to find that there were already plenty of mercantile establishments. He ventured farther west—eight miles to be exact—where he had the good fortune to meet J.H. Voorheis, also in the mercantile business. Voorheis offered Thatcher a junior partnership in his new general store in Denver. The store did fairly well through that winter season. In early January, a customer sparked an idea between the two partners. The man was from the growing settlement of Pueblo, in the southern portion of Colorado Territory. He mentioned that Pueblo would benefit from a general store such as Voorheis and Thatcher's had to offer. Before the end of the month, the partners had a fifty-fifty partnership. Voorheis would supply the merchandise for the new store in Pueblo, and Thatcher would operate it.

John Albert Thatcher built the mansion in 1883 for his wife, Margaret Henry Thatcher. He named it Rosemount for her love of roses. *Rosemount.*

In the summer of 1863, Thatcher loaded two wagons with supplies and merchandise and left Denver for Pueblo. It was a grueling journey, finally reaching Pueblo in eight days, on August 14, 1863. Here he started the first mercantile store on the dirt street of Santa Fe Avenue. He hung a pair of overalls and a pair of boots outside his establishment and opened for business. The store was a success from the start. Thatcher quickly gained a contract with the Bent brothers, in which he received a sutler's license to sell merchandise. He made regular trips to Bent's Fort, downstream on the Arkansas River, to deliver his supplies and merchandise.

Successful in obtaining many service contracts over the next year and a half, Thatcher barely managed to keep up with demand. He wrote a series of letters to his younger brother, Mahlon, describing the area, the people and the business opportunity. Finally, Mahlon was convinced and made the journey west to join his brother. His journal entry of February 21, 1865, reads, "On this day I left Martinsburg, Pennsylvania, for Colorado Territory."

After a long journey, Mahlon arrived in Denver along with a sister, Edna. The two Thatcher siblings used their savings to buy merchandise from Denver to stock the Thatcher store in Pueblo. Mahlon and Edna finally arrived in Pueblo to a warm welcome from John on March 19, 1865. With Mahlon's help, restocking between Denver and Pueblo was faster and cheaper, and their mercantile business flourished. When Oliver H.P. Baxter opened his general store, he soon sold out to the Thatchers and became a lifelong business partner.

The Thatchers soon expanded to a second store, a two-story adobe on the corner of Santa Fe Avenue and Fourth Street. This general store became the community center of sorts. John Thatcher became the assistant postmaster, and the mail was distributed through his general store. Thus the Thatcher store became a gathering place for the locals to exchange information and socialize. The Thatcher brothers increasingly gained the trust of the locals, and they even installed an enormous safe specifically for the use of their customers. The *Colorado Chieftain* said, "It is a marvel of beautiful and substantial workmanship and looks defiance at burglars and fire." Cattlemen, miners and businessmen alike would entrust thousands of dollars to the safekeeping of the Thatchers.

In 1866, the third Thatcher brother arrived in Pueblo. Henry C. Thatcher was the only brother to complete his education, receiving his law degree from Albany University in 1866, the same year he came to Colorado. In Pueblo, Henry joined his brothers but not in the mercantile business. At the age of thirty-four, he started his law practice and successfully organized the first school district. Over time, Henry's position and knowledge of the law helped his brothers in their various business practices as well.

Glory Days

By 1869, the brothers had ventured into the cattle business with friend and brother-in-law, Frank Bloom. In October 1867, John Thatcher opened another general store in Trinidad, operated by Bloom. Things were a bit different, and times were hard in Trinidad. With a lot of bartering going on for goods and supplies, Bloom often accepted cattle in trade for his wares.

Bloom bought land on the outskirts of Trinidad, where he ran a small, very profitable cattle ranch. Due to Bloom's growing cattle enterprise, the Thatcher brothers bought land east and west of Pueblo and north of the Arkansas River, near Charles Goodnight's ranch. Goodnight had settled north of Pueblo, along the Arkansas River, with the profits made from his infamous cattle drives known as the Goodnight-Loving Trail. The Thatchers, along with Frank Bloom, formed a partnership and became good friends with Goodnight. They slowly began buying out squatters who occupied land illegally. The partners eventually owned most of the land between Hardscrabble Creek and the St. Charles River in El Paso County of Colorado Territory.

Within a few short years, the Thatcher brothers' cattle and landholdings had increased in size, ranging from Pueblo south to the New Mexico state line. It is said that at one time, if a ranch hand rode from one end of the Thatcher ranch to the other, it would take nearly a week to travel.

By 1871, Pueblo was a booming city, ranked second in the Territory, and much of the credit goes to the enterprising Thatcher brothers. As trusted businessmen in the community, and the fact that they had the only safe in town, customers often asked either John or Mahlon to hold their cash for them. This practice increased to extending credit and even loans. The Thatchers believed in honest business and did so often with just a handshake. Soon, the large safe in the general store wasn't large enough. Realizing an economic opportunity, in 1871 the Thatchers opened the first bank in Pueblo. A privately held bank, named simply, The Thatcher Brothers Bank. An advertisement for the new bank ran in the *Colorado Chieftain* on January 26, 1871, stating, "Banking House of Thatcher Brothers. Having erected a Fire-Proof Banking House, we are now prepared to do a general banking business."

The bank did so well that Mahlon Thatcher traveled to Washington, D.C., to apply for a national bank charter. The government charter, granted on June 5, 1871, allowed the Thatchers to transition the bank's holdings into the First National Bank of Pueblo. Within fifteen years, they owned or had holdings in banks in Lake City, Ouray, Silverton, Trinidad and Las Animas. John and Mahlon, along with Henry's legal expertise, guided their banks to financial success. Through meticulous bookkeeping, strict management, long-term planning and a keen sense of economic perception and commerce, the Thatcher brothers built a financial empire beyond their dreams. During the financial panic of 1893, not one of the Thatchers' banks closed its doors. Even more remarkable, not one single loan was called in.

The forming of the First National Bank chains throughout the state was indeed the business investment that made the Thatchers millionaires. However, the brothers were well diversified with the Bloom cattle holdings as well as real estate investments, railroad holdings and mining interests. Early on, John and Mahlon had financed the first smelter in Pueblo and, along with partner Charles Boettcher, founded the Great Western Sugar Company, with factories all over the state

The Thatchers were also heavily involved in the state's politics. Henry Thatcher attended the Republican Territorial convention as the first delegate from Pueblo County in July 1868. In April 1869, he was appointed U.S. attorney for the Colorado Territory under President Grant. During the constitutional convention held in Denver in 1875, Henry Thatcher served on both the legislative and the judiciary committees that led to Colorado statehood in 1876. The following year, he became the first judge nominated to the Colorado Supreme Court. He served under the first chief justice, John W. Henry, who ironically enough, happened to be the father-in-law of his older brother John. Henry Thatcher eventually went on to be the chief justice of the Supreme Court as well. Perhaps an example of the political influence the Thatcher brothers had obtained was the Pueblo mayoral election of 1877. Mahlon Thatcher won by a slim victory—six votes—over his opponent, Oliver H.P. Baxter, who happened to be the brother-in-law of John Thatcher's wife, Margaret.

And the Rest Is History

John A. Thatcher married Margaret Henry on April 17, 1866. Margaret, the daughter of Colorado territorial judge John Henry, was just as ambitious as her father. At the age of sixteen, two years prior to her marriage, she became the first schoolteacher in Pueblo, teaching in a one-room sod house.

The couple had five children: Lenore in 1867, Lillian in 1870, John Henry in 1872, Albert in 1874 and Raymond in 1885. While Margaret was devoted to her children and her husband and his business career, she was also involved in a variety of charitable causes throughout the Pueblo community.

In 1891, John Thatcher began planning a mansion as a testament to his devotion to his beloved wife. The history of this magnificent mansion is a love story of John and Margaret Thatcher. Both were Colorado pioneers, having come west in 1859. They both had a strong work ethic, a pioneering spirit and love and admiration for the other. Thatcher named his mansion Rosemount, a tribute to Margaret and her favorite flower.

In the spring of 1889, Thatcher had purchased a large section of land just north of downtown Pueblo, on Greenwood Street. His land purchase stretched the entire block bounded by Fourteenth Street on the south, Fifteenth Street on the north, Greenwood Street to the west and Grand Avenue on the east side. This is where he would build the Rosemount mansion for his beloved wife. As John designed and developed his mansion, Margaret saw to the details of the furnishings.

Thatcher hired leading architect Henry Hudson Holly, of New York, to build his dream mansion. Construction of Rosemount finally got underway in earnest in the spring of 1891. As Holly's design of a grand mansion in the popular Richardsonian Romanesque style of the era began, the landscaping was also well underway. A low stone wall was taking shape that would surround the entire Thatcher estate, and trees were being planted.

In March 1891, the *Pueblo Chieftain* ran a short update on the construction of the Thatcher mansion, writing, "Everything possible has been done to make this a model dwelling and it goes without saying that Mr. Thatcher's new home will not only be pointed to as one of the most magnificent and beautiful residences of the city, but will be one of the finest in the West. Pueblo is rapidly becoming a city of elegant and beautiful homes."

Rhyolite pink volcanic stone, quarried in Castle Rock, was John's choice for the exterior walls of the mansion. The color would become the dominant theme, again chosen because of Margaret's favorite flower, the pink rose.

When it was completed in

Margaret Thatcher lived at Rosemount until her death in 1922. *Rosemount.*

1893, Rosemount's pink stone exterior was accented with a steeply pitched red Vermont slate roof, supported by Oregon pine rafters. The elegant structure was completed with cornerstones, chimneys, balconies and carved stone medallions. Pink sandstone was used for the foundation, enhanced with basswood and pine carvings. A particular highlight was the beautiful glass-enclosed veranda, which wrapped around the entire southeast corner of the mansion. A spacious and open area used year-round, this veranda is where Christmas would be celebrated by generations of Thatcher children.

The immaculate landscaping reflected the beauty and open space that is southern Colorado. On the grounds were a spacious two-story carriage house and a large greenhouse. The carriage house, with two sets of double doors, allowed easy access. The second floor of the carriage house, primarily used for storage, allowed access to the hayloft and also included sleeping quarters for the livery attendant. On the backside of the carriage house were stalls for the horses. The greenhouse was constructed in an L shape with a glass roof. A coal-fired furnace provided heat during the winter months.

Tall pillars were placed on either side of the circular driveway leading from Fourteenth Street to the mansion. A second entrance, accessed from Grand Avenue, followed a gently sloping hill, past the carriage house and continued on to the residence. At the main entrance, five pink Missouri granite monolithic columns graced the entryway.

The mansion, completed at a total cost of just over $96,000, included thirty-seven rooms, ten fireplaces, indoor plumbing, gas heating, electricity and natural gas lighting. The lighting system, a product of Tiffany & Company of New York, was a combination of electricity and natural gas that powered the many chandeliers and wall sconces. Water from an outdoor well was manually pumped into a large water tank in the attic. With hand-pulled chains, water would be released with natural gravity to the indoor plumbing fixtures. There were both steam heating and hot-water facilities for the kitchen and the bathrooms. For 1893, Rosemount was a marvel of modern technology.

Inside, the furnishings were the finest available and personally selected by Margaret. The smallest detail was not overlooked by her keen eye. The interior woodwork, masterfully carved, was of quality cherry, mahogany, maple and oak. Each individual room was enhanced by furnishings of matching wood, many of which were imported, and all handmade. Carpeting was of the highest quality, as were the two dozen hand-woven Persian, Oriental and Turkish rugs.

Entering the Rosemount mansion, friends, family and guests of the Thatchers were welcomed in the main hall. The hall, elegantly designed with white oak, including the oak parquet floor, provided an open and inviting atmosphere. The fireplace, the largest of ten in the mansion, included an intricately hand-carved mantle. Large mirrors were placed to reflect the elegant Tiffany chandelier and enhanced the lighting in the room. Etched glass graced the silver-plated chandeliers and included Favril globes from the famed Tiffany establishment. It is believed this particular Tiffany glass was the first in Colorado, installed in 1893. The ceiling was decorated to augment the room with hand-painted designs, including roses, framed by the high beams. From the fireplace mantles to the ceiling décor, Margaret's favorite flower is evident throughout the mansion.

Just off the main hall, a separate entrance led to the veranda from inside the residence. The décor in this room was chosen by Margaret to complement the wide view of the outdoors and was simply stunning. The room was filled with plants and flowers year-round, acquired from the greenhouse. It is no wonder that the Thatcher family decorated the Christmas tree in this room and celebrated the special holiday here.

Pocket doors led to the family's sitting room to the right of the main hall. Informal in décor, it was used daily as a room where the family gathered. The mahogany woodwork in the room, highlighted with gilt stenciled molding, included the fireplace. The furnishings of the room, including damask-covered chairs and a stone-topped table inlaid with colored marble, were all handsomely placed to complete the scheme of the room. French doors also led to the veranda.

The library also provided access to the veranda on the north side of the room. This room, dominated by the mahogany woodwork, featured large bookcases and an elaborate silver-plated fireplace. The carpet was imported oriental Bokkara. The furniture, also of dark woods, not only complemented the decor of the room but also reflected the business atmosphere John wanted to represent. The room served two purposes for the man of the house. It was where his invited male guests gathered after dinner to enjoy fine conversation with wine and cigars. The room also served as his office when the need arose. A small alcove in the library included two stained-glass windows facing the veranda at the east end of the room. Designed by Charles Booth of New York, the windows were entitled "Calm" and "Storm."

The parlor was a formal room, used specifically for entertaining guests. Here the architects again incorporated John's theme of the rose for his wife. The marble fireplace, trimmed in gold, is decorated in a delicate engraved floral design, as is the fire screen. The ivory-colored ceiling also included the rose-theme design. The woodwork chosen for this room was white oak, polished to a fine ivory color and trimmed in gold to complement the fireplace design. The walls were decorated in rose silk damask. The carpet in this room, light in color, perfectly accentuated the décor of the room. The furniture chosen incorporated the damask theme of the walls, featuring pieces of damask furniture with gilt legs. Two items placed in this room were some of the very few pieces brought from the Thatchers' previous home. The family's piano held a prominent place in the room, near the beautiful settee. Music was an important part of the Thatcher family's life. In a loving gesture to their daughter Lenore, who died in 1890, John and Margaret chose to include their daughter's harp in this room.

The dining room, the prominent room on the first floor, was simply exquisite in every way. The golden oak paneling was enhanced by a copy of an eighteenth-century mural, painted by a French artist commissioned by Louis XV, which graced three walls in the room. This is indicative of the many art pieces found throughout the mansion. The fireplace in this room, in matching golden oak, featured blue-glazed English ceramic tiles. The large dining table could be extended, accommodating thirty-six guests. A buzzer placed underneath the end of the table allowed the host to summon the servants. The dark wooden chairs, with green upholstered cushions, complemented the green velvet draperies. A built-in service table provided the staff the ease of serving the large number of dining guests. The family's beautiful hand-painted china was used only in this room.

The kitchen was built at the northwest corner of the residence where the heat of the sun was reduced, thereby allowing this room to be cooler. This was also a testament to the architects and the technology of Rosemount. A well-insulated walk-in closet, located in the butler's pantry, served as the cooling room for fresh fruits, vegetables and prepared foods. A large paneled pie safe was installed to keep pies fresh and insect-free. The kitchen was well equipped by 1893 standards. A large room, with brick walls, the area included a marble-topped table placed in the center of the room, used for food preparation. The oversized steel sink allowed for ease in washing pots and pans. A large hot-water tank was installed for this purpose. An icebox was also installed, and a delivery service arrived daily with blocks of ice. The dominating feature in the kitchen was obviously the cookstove. The enormous state-of-the-art cooking range was a specially ordered U.S. Army coal- and wood-burning stove, complete with a grilling feature. Ventilation was provided by intricate vents from the stove and grill piped through the outside brick wall. An interesting feature of this room is the communication system. A wooden box with call buttons activated a flag, which activated a bell, alerting the servant. It also contained a number of speaking tubes that were connected to several rooms in the mansion.

The most stunning feature leading to the second floor of the residence is also a testament of the love built into this marvelous home. The grand staircase, just off the main hall, was designed with golden oak and included hand-turned detailing. The carpet for the stairway was the most expensive of all the carpeting in the mansion. Silver-plated light fixtures graced the rail posts and cast glowing light on the various statues and figurines, commissioned by artist J. Causee. At the first turn of the winding staircase is a remarkable nine- by thirteen-foot stained-glass window. It is titled "Kingdoms of Nature." Animals and plants are depicted, as are heavenly angels, in the work created by Charles Booth. It was designed by John and Margaret as a loving memorial to two of their children, Lenore and Albert, who had died.

The second floor contained the family's bedrooms and guest rooms. The furniture was selected to match the particular wood chosen for each room.

The seven rooms were characteristically different, including the fireplace mantles, which reflected the personality of the room.

In keeping with the tradition of wealthy Victorian couples, John and Margaret had separate bedroom suites. John's suite, with its bright birch woodwork, matched the fireplace in the room. A large bed commanded the center of the room, with a large bureau for his clothes along one wall and a personal table and chaise lounge on another wall. A touching item hung to the left of the door. It was a hand-painted piece done by Margaret that featured her deceased daughter, Lenore, among angels calling her to heaven. The suite also included a private bathroom, with not one but two bathtubs. The second tub was a sitz tub used primarily for soaking one's backside.

Margaret's suite, also done in birch woodwork, included a stunning fireplace, with carved rose-flowered designs. The room was warm and bright, with many windows on the south wall. Her beloved flower, the rose, was incorporated in the design of the painted ceiling. The furniture selected by Margaret included a mirrored vanity and all contained mother-of-pearl detail.

Just down the hall was the bedroom of the Thatcher's only living daughter, Lillian. The woodwork in this room was a light colored maple, which was particularly brilliant with the sunshine streaming in from the large windows. The dominant piece in the room was Lillian's four-poster canopy bed. Other pieces included a standing framed mirror, a fainting couch and a slipper chair.

The youngest Thatcher child, Raymond, was just seven years old when the family moved into the mansion. His bedroom included a large brass bed, a large dresser and mirror and a table and chair, all in matching dark maple wood.

A testament to the consideration the Thatchers had for their employees was the addition of a sewing room. Margaret would hire the best seamstresses available and allowed them to work freely in the room, which was completely furnished to serve all their needs. An 1876 sewing machine provided the seamstresses the ease to provide the family with all of their clothing, from undergarments to fine dress shirts and evening gowns. The seamstresses would also repair household linens such as draperies, tablecloths and bedsheets.

Only one bathroom was built on the second floor that was shared by Lillian, Raymond and guests, when present. The room contained the best plumbing technology of the era, a bathtub with a scallop-shell design, a sink and a mirror. The water closet next to the bathroom was intentionally built as a separate room, as was often the custom. A simple room with light-colored tiling, the flush box placed high above the toilet allowed gravity to release the water when the chain was pulled.

Rosemount's third floor contained seven rooms for additional guests and their servants. The servants used a separate back entrance and back stairway. A small bathroom was constructed at the north end of this floor. The rooms, while warm and comfortable, were quite modest in the furnishings, and all included chamber pots and wash basins. However, the servants were encouraged to add their personal accessories and make the room their own. A billiard room was built for gentlemen on the south end of the floor.

Because Rosemount had already been wired for electricity, Holly chose a central location in the mansion where he cleverly built a closet in the basement and a closet directly above that on each floor. Holly's design was to allow for the possibility of an eventual elevator from the first floor to the third floor.

In December 1894, Margaret and her daughter, twenty-three-year-old Lillian, who was home from school for the holidays, hosted an open house reception for the ladies of the Pueblo community. This was the first glimpse the public had of the fabulous Rosemount mansion. The event, held on December 20, 1894, was covered in detail in the next day's edition of the *Pueblo Chieftain*:

> *The most delightful society event of the social seasons was an afternoon reception given by Mrs. John A. Thatcher and her daughter, Miss Lillian, yesterday at their magnificent mansion on the corner of Fourteenth and Greenwood Streets. This was the first time since the house was built that the doors have been thrown open to any large assemblage and all of the its [sic] beauties were resplendent yesterday. About 225 ladies called during the afternoon. It was so arranged that the ladies arrived at different hours and were expected to remain an hour. The orchestra was stationed on the landing of the spacious stairway. The refreshments were served in the dining room which was trimmed in pink. Pink roses, pink ribbons and pink candies were tastefully arranged in the room. The lunch was elegant and was served very gracefully.*

Life at Rosemount for the Thatcher family and the servants was one of contentment yet full of activity from dawn to dusk. There were social parties, political gatherings and business meetings, not to mention family events and highlights.

John continued his various business enterprises with both of his brothers, expanding their bank holdings and cattle ranches. Margaret remained quite active in various women's groups, social activities and local charities. In

September 1905, the Southern Colorado Pioneers Association was formed, with John and Margaret as founding members, along with John's brother Mahlon and his wife, Luna.

Following her graduation from the Pueblo schools, Lillian Thatcher attended Mrs. Sutton's finishing school in Philadelphia, Pennsylvania, graduating with high honors in November 1895. After her graduation, Lillian returned to Rosemount.

John Henry, named for Margaret's father, also attended schools in Pennsylvania. On June 29, 1887, he graduated from the Jesuit College in Morrison, Pennsylvania, and went on to complete his education at Shortlidge Military Academy at Media, Pennsylvania. He returned to Pueblo, working side by side with his father, and became an officer of his father's First National Bank of Pueblo in 1901.

In April 1901, John Henry, along with four associates, incorporated the Pueblo, Colorado State Fair Association. The purpose was to promote the state's livestock businesses by exhibiting the animals to the community and potential buyers. Contests were organized with awards given to the highest quality of the livestock. The concept caught on across the state, and John Henry served as the president of the Colorado State Fair for several years.

John Henry had also married by this time. He and Ethel (McMann) were married April 9, 1902. The couple would give John and Margaret their only grandchildren. Lenore, named for John Henry's deceased sister, was born in 1903, followed by John Henry Jr., born in 1906, and Mary Alice, born in 1910.

John and Margaret's youngest child, Raymond Calvin Cresswell, attended Pueblo's Centennial Grade School and went on to further his education at St. Paul's Prep School in Concord, New Hampshire. From there, Raymond enrolled at Yale University, graduating in 1909. Following his graduation, Raymond returned to Pueblo and the family home of Rosemount, working with his father in the family's banking interests. He would live his entire life at Rosemount and eventually inherit the magnificent mansion.

"THE MOST DARING AND SENSATIONAL ROBBERY EVER COMMITTED IN PUEBLO." This was the headline in the Pueblo *Chieftain* newspaper of February 4, 1912. On the evening of Saturday, February 3, 1912, John and Margaret were enjoying some quiet family time with their son, John Henry; his wife, Ethel; and their three grandchildren. At about 10:00 p.m., Margaret excused herself and went into her bedroom. There she discovered her room in disarray, with furniture moved and dresser drawers flung on the floor. Panicked, Margaret looked for her gold-engraved jewelry case, only to discover it was missing. The Pueblo police were immediately called. They were able to ascertain that the robber or robbers entered Mrs. Thatcher's room by climbing up a wall of the mansion and onto the porch roof, where entry was gained though a window.

Policemen were sent to the train station in an effort to catch the thieves should they attempt to leave town. During the investigation, the police discovered items belonging to Margaret Thatcher discarded in various places around Pueblo. The gold-engraved jewelry case was found in an alley dumpster in the 1100 block of Grand Avenue, just three blocks south of the Rosemount mansion. On March 13, 1912, the thief was caught. Robert Burke, twenty-five years old, was arrested in Butte, Montana. He had sold several of the Thatcher family jewels to a local saloonkeeper by the name of Robert Burgess. Unbeknownst to Burgess, he was under surveillance by local law enforcement for just such criminal activity. Several of the stolen Thatcher diamonds were recovered at a house of ill repute with ties to Burgess. The authorities arrested Burgess, who in turn incriminated Burke. In the end, Burke was convicted of felony robbery and sentenced for a term of six years in the Colorado State Penitentiary. The theft of the jewelry from the Thatcher home, estimated at $10,000, included many family heirlooms that were never recovered.

In 1912, Pueblo had become the second-largest city in the state, due in no small measure to John Thatcher and his brothers. Thatcher, at the age of seventy-five, still went to the bank everyday, where he and his brother, Mahlon, were always the first to arrive for the day's work and the last to leave each evening.

The day of Friday, June 6, 1913, began as any typical day at the bank for John Thatcher. However, by mid-morning, John became ill and could not finish his day's work. His son Raymond, also working that day at the bank, took his father home. John's doctors, aware of his failing heart, confined him to his bed and checked on him daily. Over the summer, his health seemed to improve, and the doctors allowed him leave his bed but not the mansion. On August 14, 1913, as John and Raymond were enjoying a chat, John died.

The funeral was held at Rosemount. The service, conducted by Reverend C.W. Weyer, was held in the parlor. The casket, covered with a beautiful blanket of American Beauty roses, was placed in the center of the room. Following the funeral service, the casket was taken by a hearse, followed by three automobiles, to Pueblo's Roselawn Cemetery. The largest burial ceremony ever conducted at Roselawn included members of the Southern Colorado Pioneers Association, the Sons of Colorado and businessmen of the Pueblo community. Out of respect for the man who did so much for the town, all businesses in Pueblo were closed during the ceremony. During the burial service, Reverend Weyer offered the following remarks on the life of John A. Thatcher: "The material prosperity enjoyed by this entire community today was made possible by men like John A. Thatcher, who laid the financial foundation of the city upon a sound basis, in making a fortune for himself he helped to make an empire rich."

Life at Rosemount continued on for the family after John's death. Margaret remained in the family home and eventually returned to working with her various charitable causes. During World War I, she acquired and donated a fully equipped field ambulance to the Pueblo unit of the Ambulance Corps in the memory of her late husband.

Raymond continued his father's work in both banking and the many ranching enterprises, his real passion. John's only living daughter, Lillian, also remained in the family home until her marriage in June 1915. She was forty-five years old when she entered into matrimony.

The wedding of Lillian Thatcher and Forest Rutherford was held at Rosemount, in the same parlor room as her father's funeral two years previously and also performed by Reverend C.W. Weyer. The married couple moved to Arizona, where Rutherford worked as superintendent of a large mining company.

In early March 1922, seventy-four-year-old Margaret suffered a mild heart attack. Seeking professional treatment, she traveled by train to Philadelphia, Pennsylvania, to see a group of heart specialists. Her chauffeur had driven her to the Pueblo train station in her new limited edition 1922 Pierce Arrow limousine. She was immediately hospitalized in Philadelphia, and her three children were notified. On March 18, 1922, Margaret died with her children at her bedside. The children took their mother's body back to Pueblo by train. The funeral was held at Rosemount in the parlor where her husband's funeral had been held, as well as her daughter's wedding. Internment was at Roselawn Cemetery next to her husband in the Thatcher family plot. The *Pueblo Chieftain* noted the passing of Margaret Thatcher:

> *Her life was centered around her husband and her children, to whom she was devotedly attached and in all things her home, its duties, and its responsibilities occupied her first thought and attention. Hers was a strong, ardent character, combined with a sweet, gentle, kindly spirit, forming a wholesome, just and splendid woman. Her whole life was free from ostentation; she gave generously, freely but quietly without display; as a rule her charities were known only to her immediate family.*

In 1924, Lillian returned to her family home of Rosemount after her divorce from Rutherford. She eventually became active in various charitable organizations, taking on her mother's passion. She was instrumental in providing scholarships for many in the Pueblo school system. Lillian remained at Rosemount until her death in 1948.

John Henry, the Thatcher's oldest son, died in 1928. He left behind his wife, Ethel, and three children.

Raymond, the youngest living Thatcher child, was elected to the board of directors of his father's bank following the death of John Thatcher. In 1916, he was elected as vice-president of the bank. He served as vice-president and chairman of the board until 1951.

When Raymond died at the age of eighty-three in 1968, he was the sole heir of the Rosemount mansion. His vast estate was distributed between his nieces and nephew, John Henry's children.

Through the efforts of John Henry's children, in loving memory of the Thatcher family heritage and history of Pueblo, the Thatcher Foundation was formed and the Rosemount mansion was donated to the City of Pueblo, who in turn, donated the property to the Metropolitan Museum Association.

Today

In 1969, a public trust, with support provided by members of the Thatcher family, was established to create a museum within the family walls of the Rosemount mansion.

Perhaps one of the state's finest examples of rich Victorian yesteryear is also Colorado's best-kept secret. The Rosemount Museum, the jewel of the southern plains, is resplendent in its family history and a testament to the Colorado pioneer heritage.

Visitors to Rosemount, in the center of Pueblo's historic residential center, are treated to a guided tour of the mansion and the history of the family who called it home for seventy-five years.

A testament to the quality of this magnificent mansion is the fact that most of the furniture, including the upholstery, is original to the home and over one hundred years old.

Lenore Thatcher's harp still dominates the parlor room, and the nineteenth-century settee, brought from the Thatchers' previous home, has its own special place in the parlor.

The parlor room was the scene of Lillian Thatcher's wedding, as well as the funerals of both John Thatcher and Margaret Thatcher. *Wark Photography.*

The dining room is resplendent in Victorian décor. *Wark Photography.*

The kitchen retains many of the original state-of-the-art appliances installed in 1893. *Wark Photography.*

The library contains nearly 1,700 books acquired by the family over the years and also includes a small safe table Raymond brought to the house in later years. An interesting piece in this room is a nineteenth-century Morris chair that reclines and the library chair, which, when unfolded, becomes a stepladder, handy for reaching the higher bookshelves.

The dining room is set for a formal dinner as the Thatchers would have had, complete with Margaret's china, glassware and silver. A special feature in this room is a display of five hand-painted china pieces created by Margaret.

On the second floor, the master suite and Margaret's bedroom are perhaps the most changed from the original design and furnishings. A very practical and sensible reason exists for the changes. Following the death of John Thatcher in 1913, Raymond moved into his father's room. John's original bed was replaced by a large brass bed. To showcase the few pieces of family furniture brought into the mansion from their previous home, the museum staff placed their plainer bureau against a wall in this room.

After Margaret died in 1922, her bedroom remained unchanged until Lillian returned to the mansion following her divorce in 1924. At that time,

Rosemount Block. *Rosemount Museum.*

Lillian moved into her mother's room and redecorated to suit her tastes. The primary changes were in the rugs and curtains.

Raymond and Lillian's original bedrooms have also been altered to reflect the changes in the household. While Lillian's original room has new curtains and the canopy above the bed no longer exists, Raymond's room now displays his various diplomas and photos of him during his school days.

The second-floor guest room remains in the original condition as constructed and decorated, the only such room in the museum. The sewing room reflects the many changes to the mansion over the years. In the mid-1960s, Raymond turned this room into a TV room. The museum staff carefully returned it to its original state. Because of the purpose of the room, the floor was never carpeted. However, probably due to strong cleaning solutions, the floorboards and basins have been heavily damaged, as have been the legs of the framed mirror. The original sewing machine remains.

The Rosemount Museum offers tours of the mansion every half hour and discounts to groups over ten. Special events are held throughout the year, and the mansion is available for indoor and outdoor weddings, a model business plan and community effort John Thatcher would have approved.

Fun Facts

- John A. Thatcher arrived in the small settlement of Pueblo on August 14, 1863. He died in the Rosemount mansion on August 14, 1913, exactly fifty years to the day.
- While Rosemount was wired for electricity, the local power plant shut down at 9:00 p.m. Thus, the gas lighting in the mansion served during the evening hours.
- There are many chandeliers in Rosemount; however, none are "crystal chandeliers." There are two reasons for this. While the Thatchers could obviously afford such a luxury, they were not a flamboyant couple. The second reason is that while the mansion was wired for electricity, the low voltage was not enough to power the many light bulbs.
- The doorknobs throughout the mansion are of high quality and often decorated to match the room. However, the doorknobs of the servant's rooms are plain and of lesser quality. Even more interesting are the doors to the kitchen and the dining room. The difference in the doorknobs marks the servants' side of the door from the kitchen and the family's side of the door in the dining room.
- The closets in the bedrooms of the mansion have no hanging rods. The first clothes hanger was invented and patented in 1897, four years after Rosemount was built. The first durable clothes hanger was patented in 1900.
- An example of a daily menu at Rosemount in 1900 from the Rosemount Auxiliary cookbook included the following: "Breakfast—Stewed Prunes, Oat Flakes, Frizzled Beef, Potato Puffs, Grilled Salt Pork, Sally Lunn, Toast, Coffee. Luncheon—Roast Beef Pie with Potato Crust, Fried Tripe, Hominy Croquettes, Olives, Light Biscuit, Jelly Puddings, Chocolate. Dinner—Celery Soup, French Stew, Potato Puffs, Brain Cutlets, Mashed Turnips, Pickled Cabbage, Golden Cream Cake, Orange Coconut Salad, Nuts, Raisins, Coffee."
- Rosemount was placed on the National Register on July 30, 1974, 5PE.491.

Contact Information

ROSEMOUNT MUSEUM
419 West Fourteenth Street
Pueblo, Colorado 81002
www.rosemount.org
(719) 545-5290

Chapter 9
MIRAMONT CASTLE—MANITOU SPRINGS—1895

MOUNTAIN MYSTERY AND MYSTIQUE

The Beginning

Native American tribes, primarily the Utes, roamed the base of Pikes Peak, land they called home for hundreds, if not thousands, of years. It was here in the valleys and box canyons nestled along the foothills of the great mountain that the Native Americans came for the spring season, great hunting and the spiritual guidance and rejuvenation of the boiling waters, which held special powers. The Ute Indians regarded the springs as a sacred area for centuries, originally naming the area *Manitou*, meaning "Great Spirit." Here the Ute Indians paused for guidance before continuing their annual hunting trips and farther travel up through the great Ute Pass.

Into this Indian sacred land of the Manitou and Shining Mountain, later renamed by the white man as Pikes Peak, came the explorers, trappers, traders and, eventually, the settlers. It was the era of Manifest Destiny. Explorer and frontiersman George F. Ruxton, who spent many years in the area and even had a creek named in his honor, later wrote, "And although it was Ute territory, it was neutral. When other tribes came to the springs, it was understood that there would be no fighting and no war. The tribes would come to commune with Great Spirit and partake of the healing waters. And then they, too, would leave."

The main trail used by these men was the original trail made by the Ute Indians, Ute Pass. Following a few famous westward expeditions, including

Lieutenant Zebulon Montgomery Pike's southwest exploration in 1806, a steady stream of explorers and travelers, including John C. Fremont, the "Pathfinder of the West," passed through the area on what is now known as Fremont's Trail. Reports of the spring waters and their medicinal qualities brought many travelers, including frontiersman Daniel Boone's grandson, Colonel A.G. Boone, who spent the winter of 1833 in the area specifically for the natural spring waters.

By 1868, general interest in both the area and the natural mineral waters brought a survey crew for the Kansas Pacific Railway. Leading the group was Civil War veteran General William Jackson Palmer and his right-hand man, Dr. William A. Bell. During their surveying for the railroad, the duo realized the advantages of the region and the obvious draw of the natural waters. By 1872, Palmer had formed the Fountain Colony and began plans for the future town of Colorado Springs, while Bell built a home up Ute Pass.

On a steep hillside just above the new town site, Father Jean Baptiste Francolon began building a Tudor Queen Anne structure that would become a majestic edifice filled with mystery and mystique. Jean Baptiste Francolon was born in 1854 to wealthy parents in the Clermont region of France. He was the only child of Jacques and Marie Francolon. Both Jacques and Marie were from prominent families. Jacques's grandfather Colonel Mari Francolon was a Castilian of Barcelona, Spain. Marie Plagne Francolon, born in Beaulieu, France, was the daughter of Count de Chalembelles, who served under Napoleon I.

Jacques Francolon was an aristocratic diplomat in the French government and later served as the French consul in what is now known as Moscow. As Jean grew older, he was sent to the best private schools. Considered a brilliant student, Jean excelled in his studies, receiving high marks in all subjects. He studied with the Jesuit fathers in Paris, where he eventually realized his spiritual calling. Following his schooling, his father secured a position for Jean in the French embassy.

However, Jean had other plans and chose to enter the priesthood. Through a recommendation from his bishop and following a required exam, Jean entered the seminary at St. Sulpice, France. In 1878, twenty-four-year-old Jean Baptiste Francolon was sent to the United States, where he served as secretary to Bishop Jean Lamy, the first Catholic bishop in New Mexico Territory, where Jean Baptiste Francolon was later ordained as a priest. He later became chancellor of the Archdiocese of Santa Fe.

In 1881, Father Francolon made his final trip to Rome, following the death of his father. He and his mother returned to Santa Fe in March 1881. Despite all of Father Francolon's humanitarian efforts, hostility remained among the old Spanish Catholic Church and the new French Catholic Church. During this period of unrest, Father Francolon was actually poisoned. While drinking from his chalice during mass on a warm July morning in 1885, the father fell ill. It was determined that poison of some sort was mixed in with the contents of the chalice. Although he eventually recovered, the incident affected his health for the rest of his life.

In March 1892, Father Francolon was assigned as the pastor of Our Lady of Perpetual Help in Manitou Springs. This particular parish was founded by Bishop Joseph Projectus Machebeuf, a dear friend of Father Jean Lamy. Machebeuf, who arrived in the Colorado area in 1860, was responsible for establishing a large and strong Catholic community in the Rocky Mountain West. It was a blessing to Francolon, as he believed the Manitou healing waters, along with the fresh mountain air, would restore his health issues. He fell in love with the beautiful pristine setting and brought his mother, Marie, along with him. The April 23, 1892 issue of the *Manitou Journal* published an article on the father's arrival:

> *Rev. J.B. Francolon, formally of Santa Cruz, has been appointed to take charge of the Catholic parish here in place of Father Frederick Bender, who has been called to Colorado Springs. A recent issue of the* Santa Fe Daily New Mexican *contains a very kind and flattering notice of the Reverend Father. Says the* New Mexican*: "While regretting to lose so good a man from the midst, Santa Feans nevertheless will be pleased to learn of his promotion. Rev. Francolon is a most charming and talented gentleman, and a man of broad views."*

Later that year, Francolon built a home for himself and his mother on Capitol Hill Avenue. Father Francolon purchased the property in his mother's name. An article appeared in the September 17, 1892 issue of the *Manitou Journal* reporting, "Father Francolon will erect a handsome $3,500 cottage on Capitol Hill this Fall." A second lot was purchased just below Father Francolon's first lot. This particular section of land was once a parcel of land owned by one of Colorado's most controversial citizens, Colonel John M. Chivington, the commanding officer who led the horrific attack on an Indian village in Colorado Territory on November 29, 1864, known in history as the Sand Creek Massacre. The earliest land deeds recorded list Chivington as the landowner in 1862. El Paso County land records reveal that Chivington sold the land in 1867 through his son-in-law, who had power of attorney. However, Chivington, believing he was a victim of land fraud, took his case to court, claiming that he had given no such power of attorney. The lawsuit dragged on for years, with Chivington eventually losing the court case. Defiant and undaunted, he took the case to the Colorado Supreme Court, where he again lost in 1886. The land was sold to the Colorado Springs Company, founded by General William Jackson Palmer. Palmer later sold the land to the city of Manitou Springs.

Following Father Francolon's purchase of the land, he employed the Gillis brothers, Angus and Archie, who had constructed Our Lady of Perpetual Help Catholic church, to build his dream home. He also enlisted the services of local stonemason William Frizzell. According to the daughter of Angus Gillis, Father Francolon presented his architectural designs to Frizzell and the Gillis brothers. After hours of discussion, Francolon came to trust the Gillis brothers and Frizzell. This was important to Francolon, as he had spent many hours drawing his plans based on architectural wonders he had seen from his years of traveling the world with his diplomat father.

Construction began in the fall of 1895. Frizzell used hand-cut native green sandstone to build the castle's two-foot-thick walls. This unique stone was quarried along Fountain Creek. The European-style castle, predominately designed in the Queen Anne style, emerged over a two-year period. It was a stunning structure with nine separate styles of architecture, including English Tudor, Elizabethan, Byzantine, Moorish, Romanesque and Venetian styles. A Chateau style was used in the half-timber accents to the sandstone structure, added randomly throughout the four stories. The remarkable structure included castellated battlements topping the structure at each end of the castle, reminiscent of medieval European castles. Gothic Flemish stepped gables enhanced the exterior. Francolon explained his eclectic style, saying, "Romanesque style was too uniform, Ionic too classic for romantic Manitou, Gothic too pious for a residence, Moorish too pagan for a clergyman, and Colonial out of order for a mountain region."

As the construction of Manitou Springs' finest residence progressed, the *Manitou Springs Journal* reported on the progress periodically throughout the year. In the November issue, the publication wrote glowingly of the new edifice, proclaiming it to be "one of the handsomest and most artistic buildings in Colorado."

Early in the construction process, Father Francolon recruited a group of the Religious Order of the Sisters of Mercy to open a sanitarium in his former home. The father's idea was to provide care to ailing priests and nuns of limited means. Because of the natural mineral springs, the healing properties

Miramont exterior, 1897. *Miramont Museum.*

and Father Francolon's improved health, he believed the water, the mountain air and the sisters' nurturing ways would be of great advantage to those who were suffering. Father Francolon donated his home to the sisters with the understanding that the sisters would also look after the needs of Francolon and his mother, such as cooking, cleaning and laundry. The *Manitou Springs Journal* broke the story of the father's donation on the front page of its July 13, 1895 issue with the headline "GIFT TO SISTERS OF MONTCALME."

The sisters moved a group of patients into the former Francolon home. They named their care facility Montcalme Sanitarium. Mother Mary Baptiste Meyers, the Mother Superior of Colorado, opened the sanitarium, which received its first patients in August.

However, Bishop Matz, of the Denver Diocese, who was responsible for bringing Father Francolon to the Manitou Springs parish, was not receptive to the idea. In a letter dated August 8, 1895, Matz wrote Father Percy A. Phillipps, founding pastor of Denver's St. Joseph Redemptorist parish and chaplain of the Good Shepherd Home, saying that he had assured "the Sisters of Charity and the Sisters of St. Francis that neither a hospital nor Sanitarium be started for some time within Manitou or Colorado Springs. There is absolutely no necessity for any such institution in Manitou. Both in justice to the existing institutions with whom it would necessarily interfere and in justice to the Sisters of Mercy who would make a bad investment. I cannot allow this."

It seems as if a bit of mishandled financial donation occurred during this time. A French friend of Father Francolon's, Viscount Peufeilhoux, sent a monetary donation to the father to be used for the Hospital of St. Francis in Colorado Springs. Unfortunately, the money did not arrive in time, and construction of the hospital was stalled. When the money finally arrived, the good father chose to invest the money by purchasing eight thousand shares in the Moose Gold Mining Company. In January 1896, Peufeilhoux sent another donation to Francolon to be used for the Sisters of Mercy's Montcalme Sanitarium.

The following year, Peufeilhoux, unhappy with the stock returns from the Moose Gold Mining Company, wrote a bizarre letter to Bishop Matz accusing Father Francolon of investing his money in the mining company without his consent and then stating that the father had overcharged him for the shares in the mining company. Father Francolon responded with a letter addressed to Bishop Matz, dated May 29, 1897, stating that his correspondence with Peufeilhoux would provide:

[M]y best advocate and will condemn the Viscount, at the very least, of a total forgetfulness of all he has said to me and especially written. The Viscount has threatened me for such a long time that my lawyers are ready both for the defense and the prosecution, and now that he has done all in his power, by writing to my bishop, to ruin my reputation, and my future, and especially to tarnish my character, I feel no pity for him. But I leave to God the care to avenge me.

Receiving both letters, Matz proved to be Francolon's avenger. In a letter to Viscount Peufeilhoux, dated September 10, 1897, Matz responded by stating that Peufeilhoux's allegations were contradictory in nature and thereby exonerated Father Francolon from any wrongdoing.

Within six months, the Sisters of Mercy organization expanded to receive tubercular patients, the all-too-common dreaded ailment of the nineteenth century. Father Francolon filled the need for care for these patients. On August 1, 1895, Francolon sold an adjacent lot to the sisters for $3,000, at 5 percent interest.

Glory Days

Francolon's original four-story castle was literally built into a steep sloping hillside. With such construction, the rear of the castle was heavily fortified against the hill. Each of the four floors was built in a "stair-stepping" manner up the hillside. This allowed the Gillis brothers to provide at least one exit on each floor to level ground. There were ten entrances to the castle. The main entrance, through a beautiful Gothic arched oak door, was under the magnificent porte cochere. Later that year, Francolon completed an east-wing addition to the castle.

Inside the twenty-two-inch-thick castle walls, fourteen thousand square feet of medieval wonder lent to the mystique, with sixty windows and forty-six rooms, each one unique and with Francolon's personal eclectic style. Many of the rooms were built with eight sides, and only a few rooms were built with four square corners. A library and chapel on the second story were octagonal, while a third-floor guest room was built with sixteen sides. A gallery, also on the third floor, included a unique display of Native American artifacts and the Francolons' European tapestry collection.

Several rooms had arched doors and windows. Fir and pine were the predominant decorative wood used throughout the castle. Lavish furnishings in the castle were enhanced by beautiful tapestries, lace curtains and European statuary. The grand staircase rising through three of four floors included three sixteen-foot windows and two arched windows, each in a different architectural style. A separate, narrow, four-story staircase led to the rooms where the servants slept in small, sparsely furnished quarters. While the castle included indoor plumbing and steam heating, eight fireplaces were also included in the design.

The reception hall on the second floor was described in the *Denver Republican* newspaper as "furnished in pale cream and blue." The *Evening Telegraph* newspaper described Father Francolon's expensive European paintings, the dominating features of the room, "including the much admired St. Bruno of Velasquez, a small masterpiece more valuable to the priest than the house itself. Other pieces of art are *Gregory the Great, Our Lady of Guadaloupe* and *The Virgin Child*."

In the reception hall, a massive eleven-foot-tall and sixteen-foot-wide red stone fireplace, considered at the time to be the largest fireplace in the country, warmed the room. This fireplace was built seven feet into the side of the back hillside. The chimney extended along the back of the castle through three floors, allowing for a fireplace on each of the ascending floors. Constructed of nearly twenty tons of red sandstone and topped by African mahogany, the fireplace dominated a room filled with velvet-and-brocade-upholstered chairs and sofas and marble-topped tables. An alcove, connected to the room with a Moorish arch, included a square grand piano. Wall sconces provided light to the room. Just off this room, double doors led to the conservatory, which opened out to a veranda.

Also on the second floor were two dining rooms. Father Francolon's smoking room was located between a small private dining room with a curved wall at one end and the formal eight-sided dining room. The serving kitchen was connected to the dining room, where Marie Francolon's French servants served the meals prepared by the Sisters of Mercy at the Montcalme facility. The meals were delivered from the Montcalme Sanitarium through an underground tunnel leading to the Miramont Castle.

Father Francolon included an unusual concept in his architectural design. Several tunnels were constructed under the castle. It is believed the tunnels were built as escape routes. This is a plausible explanation, as the Francolon family lived through the French revolution. Another unique feature to the castle was a secret passageway that ran the entire length of the second floor.

The third floor included a seven-sided glass solarium with an eighteen-foot crowned-glass ceiling. This floor was the location of Francolon's extensive art collection, including rare paintings, tapestries and Native American art. Five exquisite Moorish keyhole stained-glass windows grace the west end of this floor. The guest accommodations included a unique sixteen-sided guest room with closets and a bathroom. The fireplace in this room was made of solid brass.

Marie Francolon's original bedroom proved to be too small to accommodate her thirteen-foot-tall French solid mahogany four-poster bed, reportedly once owned by France's Empress Josephine. Thus, the father's original library, next to this room, was converted into his mother's bedroom suite. Marie's original bedroom became her dressing room. The hexagonal room, with access to a private bathroom, was decorated in peach and cream colors, accented in oak trim. The fireplace in this room, decorated in tile, was later reported by the Sisters of Mercy to have a secret compartment. A large stone archway led to Father Francolon's sleeping quarters. It was a simple room, reflecting the father's character. The only luxury was a private bathroom.

The fourth floor included the tower room with splendid views of the mountains, as well as the town below. The servants' quarters were on this floor, including Marie Francolon's personal French servants. A series of small

An 1898 view of the reception hall. *Miramont Museum.*

The restored reception hall as it looks today. *Miramont Museum.*

Mrs. Francolon's huge dark oak bed, thirteen feet tall, must have been a challenge to get up the staircase to the second floor. *Miramont Museum.*

Mrs. Francolon's room as it looks today. *Miramont Museum.*

rooms and closets served as storage space for a variety of things, including linens and draperies, which were changed in the castle during the summer and fall seasons.

The grounds of the castle included a conservatory, a greenhouse, a chapel and a garden. The garden included stone retaining walls built by local stonemason William Frizzell. Mountain flora and greenery were planted and cared for by the father's servants.

When the castle was completed in 1897, Father Francolon moved into the new home. Francolon christened the castle Miramont, which means "look at the mountain." The *Denver Republican* reported on the completion of the castle in its February 23, 1897 issue:

> *Miramont castle was built last year by Father Francolon after months of deep study of which style of architecture should be adopted as better suited to the locality. So it was decided by the reverend clergyman to take some of the Romanesque, Gothic, Moorish and Middle Ages style and blend them so artistically together as to give at once satisfaction to the eyes and make it appear as though built on the border of France and Spain, countries in which Father Francolon traces far back [to] his ancestors. No architects were employed, as it was feared few would understand exactly what was wanted. The plans were drawn by Father Francolon himself, every detail given ear and attention, and the work superintended by him alone from the beginning to the end.*

And the Rest Is History

On February 22, 1897 Father Francolon held a charity event at Miramont to raise funds for the purchase of land for a public library in Manitou Springs. A festive colonial costume ball with three hundred in attendance was a complete success. The *Colorado Springs Gazette Telegraph* reported on the gala affair in the February 23, 1897 issue:

> *General and Martha Washington, Miles Standish, Mr. and Mrs. John Adams, Mr. and Mrs. Gov. Winthrop, Gen. Lafayette, Gen. Rochambeau, Mr. and Mrs. James Madison and many other men and women of the old and quaint days of America were represented.*
>
> *As the ninth hour was pealing the reception party assembled in the picture gallery and marched to the receiving room as the orchestra rendered "Columbia."*

Two minuets were danced by four couples each, followed by general dances participated in by all the historical characters. Most graciously and stately they tripped to and fro in unison to the music.

Six months later, Father Francolon held a second ball for charity on August 24, 1897. This event, another huge success, raised funds for poor in the community. The August 25, 1897 issue of the *Rocky Mountain News* described the castle during the "Grande Ball de Chariot" event as "one of the handsomest residence buildings in the state, and rising from a level, obtained by blasting hundreds of feet of solid rock, its upper stories nestled against natural stone walls, its towers and turrets boldly outlined against the sky, it is doubly imposing and its rugged beauty accentuated."

Father Francolon and his mother, Marie, were apparently experiencing financial difficulties, as evidenced in recently translated letters of Father Francolon's. This is most likely the situation, as not long after the completion of Miramont Castle, the Gillis brothers were forced to sue the good father for payment for their work. Father Francolon then took out a loan for $6,000 on the Miramont property to pay his hired contractors.

After living in the dream home for three short years, the Francolons suddenly abandoned their castle in 1900 and returned to their French homeland, taking valuable artwork with them. Their business affairs were handled by their attorney, George Renn. In 1902, General William Jackson Palmer donated $1,000 to help relieve the debt against the castle.

While the real reason for the Francolons' abandonment of Miramont remains a mystery, rumors were whispered in the tight mountain community. Stories circulated that Father Francolon departed amid scandal. In the winter months of 1899, a heated and sensitive confrontation occurred between the Father and the Mother Superior, Mary Baptiste Meyers. The incident is recorded in *Journal*, a book written by the Sisters of Mercy, which referred to "oral tradition among the Sisters, which in this case cannot be verified because of the shame and silence that enveloped the departure of Francolon from Manitou."

According to the *Journal* account, the Mother Superior accused the father of pedophilia, a serious accusation indeed. Father Francolon responded to the Mother Superior's accusation with uncharacteristic anger. Refuting her claim, he went on to say that she would die within the year. Somehow, the Mother Superior's accusation reached the whispering winds of the Manitou Springs community. Angus Gillis's daughter, Lenore, later related that Dr. Ogilbee raced from the Montcalme Sanitarium to the Gillis home with news of an angry mob bent on lynching the father. Angus Gillis drove a wagon to the castle, where he placed the father into the wagon, covered him with blankets and drove him past the lynch mob and into Colorado Springs and the sanctuary of the St. Mary's Catholic Church. From here, Father Francolon eventually made his way back to France. He never returned to Colorado. A few months later, his mother followed him to France, where she died four months later.

After the departure of the Francolons, Miramont Castle sat vacant for nearly four years. Following a fire that began in the furnace room of the Montcalme Sanitarium in 1904, the Sisters of Mercy, with the assistance of Dr. Geierman, purchased Miramont Castle for an undisclosed sum. Dr. Geierman urged the continued practice of Father Sebastian Kneipp's natural spring water therapy, consisting of drinking large quantities of the Manitou's mineral waters, as well as bathing in the natural waters.

For the next three years, several changes to the castle, which was only utilized in the summer months, due to the high cost of heating during the winter, were made to accommodate patients. It was during this period of change that the sisters renamed the castle "Montcalme" to carry on the familiar name. The sisters hired both the Gillis brothers, the original contractors, and William Frizzell, the original stonemason of the castle, to make the required improvements. Frizzell also had an ice delivery business that made regular deliveries to the castle. Frizzell's grandson, who often accompanied his grandfather on deliveries to the castle, later described his experiences, recounting, "The requirement of the castle was not the usual house delivery for it took a full wagon load to fill the ice box. I was always most happy to help on that delivery for though the transporting of the ice was a tedious job I was always rewarded with goodies from the icebox."

The Sisters of Mercy provided the needed care to their patients in both facilities until 1907, when an electrical fire destroyed the Montcalme Sanitarium. Sixteen patients were evacuated from the burning building, and three more, who were disabled, were carried out. The Manitou Fire Department responded and saved the nearby structures, including the homes near the structure and one of the cottages used for the isolated tubercular patients. The *Colorado Springs Gazette* newspaper covered the story in its November 5, 1907 issue, writing, "Sister Mary Alexis, on night watch, awoke almost stifled by smoke, [and] gave alarm to other Sisters. These 6 sisters did heroic work. They aroused those able to care for themselves, then carried out those unable. They carried out one paralyzed man, Mr. Dempsey, who could not make a move."

The Sisters of Mercy operated a sanitarium at Miramont Castle, which they renamed Montcalme Sanitarium. *Miramont Museum.*

The sisters moved their remaining patients into the Miramont Castle facility, where they continued to serve the health needs of the community. The third-floor seven-sided glass solarium, with its eighteen-foot crowned-glass ceiling, was used as an operating room. In 1916, the sisters considered expanding their facility to a home for needy senior citizens. It seems as if the inner factions of the organization of over forty years ago were alive and well. Responding to their request, Father G. Raber, of the St. Mary's Catholic Church in Colorado Springs, responded, stating his disapproval in a letter dated December 7, 1915: "Manitou has but little sun during the long and many winter months...and just imagine if you can the dear old, perhaps crippled to with rheumatism, men and women having to hobble up the little mountain especially on a windy day or when the paths and ways are slippery from ice. I confer, it is difficult for me to imagine such a scene and not become profane."

In 1926, the sisters, under the leadership of Sister Dolores and Sister Vincent, began taking patients with heart problems and stomach disorders. However, by 1928, the economy across the country was beginning to slide toward the Depression of the 1930s. The sisters were faced with a dual set of circumstances that eventually caused them to close the sanitarium by year's end. Financial concerns were compounded by the medical advances in treating tubercular patients. Several surgical techniques in the treatment of pulmonary tuberculosis were developed. With such advances and ongoing research, the need for such sanitariums soon became a thing of the past. The final decision rested with the apostolic delegate who advised that Montcalme Sanitarium be closed to the public.

On July 15, 1945, the archbishop of Denver, Urban J. Vehr, sent a letter to the Sisters of Mercy giving permission to sell the Manitou Springs property. In March 1946, the historic castle was sold to Alexander Gardner and John Mutton. They renamed the edifice Castle Apartments with the intent to convert the castle into apartments for returning veterans of World War II. The interior was divided into nine apartments for the families of Camp Carson soldiers.

A year later, on April 25, 1947, the two men sold the castle to Mrs. Cora W. Wood, who continued to operate the property as an apartment complex for the next eight years. It was under Wood's ownership that the building was returned to its original name, Miramont Castle. Wood sold the castle on March 28, 1953. From that date, the castle changed ownership no less than eight times.

In 1975, under the ownership of Alison E. Nadle, the building was nearly condemned by city officials.

Today

The following year, the historic castle was purchased by the Manitou Springs Historical Society. The society was able to match a grant from the Centennial-Bicentennial Commission, with a $7,000 donation from architectural heritage restoration consultant, Philip Lawrence Hannum. The society began the restoration, relying on the historic architectural assessment, documents and photographs Hannum provided. Extensive work followed, including exterior repairs such as re-grouting the chimneys and repairing the parapets. Astonishingly, 267 windows needed to be replaced. Victorian furnishings were either bought or donated as the restoration process continued. None of the original furnishings survived. For example, photos of the interior of the castle during the years it

served as apartments show both Marie's French four-poster bed and the father's piano. What became of these and the many other furnishings is not known.

Miramont Castle was opened to the public as a museum on July 8, 1976, coinciding with the celebration of Manitou Springs 100th anniversary, as well as the nation's bicentennial anniversary and just days before the 100th celebration of Colorado statehood.

Opposite: The grand staircase as it looked in 1899. *Miramont Museum.*

Above: The oak staircase to the second floor landing has been altered through renovations. *Linda Wommack.*

Restoration of the castle has continued through the years. During restoration of the Reception Hall, the back wall was opened, west of the enormous sandstone fireplace. It was discovered that the fireplace had no man-made support but rested solidly on the edge of the rock mountain. This room has been restored to the Victorian parlor room depicted in Father Francolon's original floor plans. Decorated in deep red, the room is splendidly reproduced in the style of an era of long ago. A crystal chandelier and two matching wall sconces grace the room.

The Miramont Castle is dedicated to the Victorian era. Each room is an example of life during the time in which Father Francolon and his mother lived in the castle. Visitors can witness firsthand Francolon's eclectic architecture and walk the halls of this extravagant castle. On the second floor is the chapel, restored in 1982. Handcrafted stained-glass windows were inserted. The pews in the chapel came from a small church in the San

Exterior view of Miramont in 2013. *Miramont Museum.*

Luis Valley and date to the 1890s. The original conservatory on this floor is now the Queens Parlor Tea Room, serving lunch and Victorian High Tea. According to museum curator Peggie Yager, this was the first room to be renovated. During the process, a wall was removed dating to the apartment era of the castle. This revealed a room previously unknown. The room contains a stone wall with a beautiful stone arch in the center. This archway was later enclosed with matching stone. Yager believes this may have been the tunnel entrance to the castle used by the sisters from Montcalme. This room is now used as the kitchen for the Queens Parlor Tea Room.

Also on this floor is one of the original water closets. The pull-chain commode, with an oak seat and an oak water box, is decorated in a raised pattern. The claw-foot bathtub is original, as are the faucets, drains and the metal towel rack with scrolled ends.

Miramont Castle is said to be one of the most haunted castles in the United States. Multiple witness accounts of mysterious apparitions have been reported by both staff and visitors to the castle. Accounts include ghostly visions of men, women and children in Victorian attire wandering throughout the castle. Museum staff member Bee Busch recounts an incident when she left the front counter of the gift shop. Looking up, she saw a headless woman in an ankle-length, cream-colored dress with long sleeves, a high collar and a laced-bib front moving toward her. The apparition then moved on to the Christmas Room and disappeared. The apparition of a woman dressed in Victorian attire has been seen by many gazing back through a mirror. It is somewhat ironic that an unexplained phenomenon occurs in Father Francolon's bedroom. Several members of the staff have reported indentations on the bedcovers as if someone was sitting there. Smoothing out the covers, the indentations reappear. Another ironic twist to the former home of Father Francolon is the unnerving phenomena that occur in the chapel. There are tales of objects being moved by unseen hands, mysterious voices are heard and a distinct cold spot exists in the chapel. The Christmas Room hosts the ghost of a little girl playing with a doll in the room. Several staff members and visitors have reported a feeling of unease in this room. The Doll Room is the sight of another ghostly little girl. Playing with her Victorian dolls, she seems content in her surroundings.

The sprawling, fortress-like edifice that is Miramont Castle stands today as a testament to the vision of a Catholic father and his faith in the natural waters, clean air and mountain beauty of Manitou Springs.

Fun Facts

- Father Joseph Projectus Machebeuf, who established Our Lady of Perpetual Help in Manitou Springs, which eventually brought Father Francolon to the town, was later immortalized in Willa Cather's epic novel *Death Comes for the Archbishop*.
- Father Sebastian Kneipp's practices, including drinking large quantities of the local spring water as well as bathing in spring water, were first used at Montcalme Sanitarium. Many of Kneipp's practices are still used today by practitioners of naturopathic medicine.
- Following the death of his mother, Marie, Father Francolon returned to America, spending his last ten years in New York, where he died on December 4, 1922. He is buried in that city's Archdiocese Cemetery, with a tombstone that lists his incorrect birth year.
- The location of the cottage and original Montcalme Sanitarium is now the upper parking lot of Miramont Castle. The stone wall on

the north and west side of this parking lot is all that remains of the original cottage.

- Throughout the restoration process, reproductions of 1896 vintage wallpaper were used. However, there is a piece of original wallpaper located in the back of a small closet under the Grand Stairway.
- The Tea Room seating area was originally a veranda. In 1982, grill panels were installed on the deck and a gate was fashioned from the original jailhouse door from the 1902 Cripple Creek jail.
- Located on the far back corner of the upper parking lot of Miramont Castle is the last remaining tubercular hut originally constructed by the Sisters of Mercy. Patients who required isolation lived in the hut during their stay for treatment.
- Miramont Castle was placed on the National Register on April 11, 1977, REP.204.

Contact Information

MIRAMONT CASTLE
9 Capitol Hill Avenue
Colorado Springs, Colorado 80829
www.miramontcastle.org
(719) 685-1011

Chapter 10

THE CHEESMAN-EVANS-BOETTCHER
MANSION—DENVER—1908

FIT FOR A GOVERNOR

The Beginning

In 1908, the new red brick mansion with fine white columns at the southeast corner of Eighth Avenue and Logan Street was one of the finest on fashionable Capitol Hill. Built by a self-made millionaire who didn't live to see its completion, the dwelling became the home of the first territorial governor's grandson, and still later, it would be owned by a wealthy Denver businessman. This fabulous Denver mansion has a storied history unlike any other.

When thirty-five-year-old Walter Scott Cheesman, a druggist by trade, arrived in Denver City on July 10, 1861, he rode in on an oxcart from Chicago. During the first few months of the Pikes Peak gold rush, two of Cheesman's brothers preceded him to Denver City, where they opened a drugstore at the corner of Blake and F Streets (today's Fifteenth Street). However, the high altitude and dry climate did not agree with the first two Cheesman brothers, and they returned to their home state of New York. When W.S. Cheesman arrived with his oxcart loaded with wares and supplies, he restocked the store, made a few changes and reopened. Cheesman soon became popular with his customers and many Denver businessmen. Several businesses rented space in the brick Cheesman building, including the Kountze brothers, who operated a primitive bank, trading in gold dust, from the back half of the building. Later, their enterprise would become the Colorado National Bank. The generosity and goodwill that Cheesman extended to his fellow businessmen did not go unnoticed. In fact, the Denver businessmen honored him in November 1861 for his customer service and great kindness for "preparing prescriptions by the city physician at 'cost or near cost.'" An ardent promoter of Denver and its future, he aligned himself with many leaders, politicians and organizations. In 1868, he was instrumental in forming the Denver Gas Company. It was about this time that Cheesman sold his drugstore, later stating to a group of businessmen that he, "just had too many irons in the fire to fill prescriptions."

The following summer of 1869, Cheesman, along with Territorial Governor John Evans and Denver businessman David H. Moffat, worked to build a rail line from the railroad yards in Cheyenne, Wyoming, to Denver for their Denver Pacific Railroad Company. By the summer of 1870, the Denver Pacific track was finished, and the first freight engine, the Walter S. Cheesman, rolled into Denver from Cheyenne. In a symbolic gesture to Cheesman and his significant achievement in bringing railroad service to Denver, several bystanders and staff members of the First National Bank, which operated in Cheesman's building, gathered on the rooftop of the brick building, cheering as the train rolled into town.

Cheesman's partnership with Evans and Moffat would prove to be the trifecta in many of Denver's enterprises from banking to real estate, water and gas. The trio continued to form several more railroad companies, including the Denver and Boulder Valley Railroad Company in 1870 and the Denver and South Park Railway Company in 1872.

Then, in the autumn of 1879, several members of the various railroad companies formed the Union Depot and Railroad Company in a consolidated effort to build one central depot in Denver. On November 24, 1879, the elected officers included Walter S. Cheesman as president. Cheesman successfully negotiated for twelve acres of land on the west side of Wynkoop Street, between Sixteenth and Eighteenth Streets. Before the year was out, plans were in development for Denver's Union Passenger Station.

It was during this time that Cheesman began buying vacant land in Denver. The nationally acclaimed credit reporting company of R.G. Dunn and Company stated that Cheesman had a net worth of $250,000 and was "one of the staunchest investors."

Among Cheesman's many contributions to Denver was his involvement in the Denver Library Association in 1873, and in 1875, he was among the founding members of the Colorado Stock and Exchange Board, serving as one of the chairmen.

Walter Scott Cheesman began the construction of his mansion in the fashionable Capitol Hill neighborhood in 1907. *Denver Public Library.*

Another event in Cheesman's life was of a personal nature. Following the tragic death of his first wife and two-year-old son, Cheesman had remained single. In 1873, the forty-seven-year-old widower married a delightful Denver woman who was herself a widow, Alice Foster Sanger. Two years later, the couple became the proud parents of a daughter they named Gladys.

Perhaps his greatest achievement, to the great benefit of Denver residents, was his involvement in the Denver City Water Company. Organized in 1870 with Colonel James Archer as president and Moffat as treasurer, Cheesman served on the board of directors. With the advent of rail service to Denver, the city's population naturally grew. Cheesman saw the need for additional water supplies to the arid city.

In March 1889, the Citizens' Water Company was formed by a group of citizens concerned for the future of Denver's water supply. Among the founding members was Walter Cheesman. On November 22, 1889, the City of Denver issued Ordinance #119 to Cheesman's water company, authorizing the company to lay water lines throughout the city. Two years later, Cheesman and his company began the construction of the Cheesman Dam. In the hills southwest of Denver, in Platte Canyon, this dam captured water from the South Platte River. The water then flowed to the water company facilities in Denver through a series of underground pipes. The high demand required the company to lay additional piping a year later. The Cheesman Dam and water supply was a marvel of 1890 engineering. Nearly three million cubic yards of stone and cement were used to build the dam, which was the highest in the world at the time.

As if building dams and railroads wasn't enough for Walter Cheesman, in September 1891 he became the first vice-president of Denver's esteemed

First National Bank, a position he held until his death. Quite active in Denver society, he was among the founders of the Denver Club in 1880.

With his various land purchases over the years, Cheesman also became very successful in the development of real estate in the growing, prosperous town of Denver. His first real estate venture was the purchase of two entire blocks of vacant land in 1883 from Henry C. Brown. The land Cheesman bought was between Broadway and Lincoln Street and Sixteenth Street and Colfax Avenue. He later sold one block of this land to the state of Colorado. The other block, known as the Cheesman Block, was designated as open space by the city. Occasionally Cheesman allowed select groups to use his open space for venues, such as the organizers of the Festival of Mountain and Plain and the Gentleman's Driving and Riding Club. A set of bleachers was built for the spectators.

By 1900, Cheesman was one of the largest owners of several parcels of Denver's prime real estate. In 1901, he bought sixteen vacant lots in Denver's elite residential area of Capitol Hill. The lots were situated along Eighth Avenue and included the corner lot at Logan Street. It was at this location that Cheesman began the construction of a second mansion for he and his wife, Alice, and his daughter, Gladys. Little did he know this would one day be home to the state's governors.

Glory Days

To build his grand home, Cheesman hired architects Aaron Gove and Thomas Walsh in 1907 to design his mansion. Meanwhile, Cheesman had sold his first mansion and rented the home of recently deceased Denver attorney Mitchell Benedict, located at 1200 Pennsylvania Street. From this location, he placed his orders for the best building materials available, including a large quantity of bricks, specially kilned in a deep red color, to achieve the design of the quality Georgian Revival mansion.

With construction of the mansion's foundation completed, landscapers were hired to plant trees and shrubs on the east end of the property. Unfortunately, later that year, Walter Cheesman died.

After a time, Mrs. Alice Cheesman and her daughter, Gladys, renewed the construction of the mansion. They hired Denver architects Willis A. Marean and Albert J. Norton to complete the work. The new architects incorporated Cheesman's original design with a few changes made by Mrs.

The Cheesman mansion as it appeared shortly after completion. *Denver Public Library.*

Cheesman. The result, completed in 1908, was a grand addition to Denver high society. From the outside, the brick home, surrounded by wrought-iron fencing and brick posts, was quite pleasing. The deep red brick, enhanced with white wood and climbing ivy along the walls, presented an elegant style to the three-story mansion. Roman columns graced the west portico up to the second-story widow's walk. The handsome arched windows were the final exterior touches. The view from the street met with citywide approval.

Inside, it was the dramatic one-hundred-foot-long entry hall with a broad columned corridor that spoke to the elegance of the mansion. Ornate eighteenth-century French chandeliers provided light along the long foyer, which led to the large reception hall. This, in turn, opened into a large library. To the left of this room was a large parlor, which opened to a palatial dining room with walls of solid walnut. The semicircular sunroom led outdoors to the perfectly manicured lawn. This was the area where many social events occurred.

The magnificent wide staircase led to the rooms on the second and third floors. The central living quarters for the family, on the second floor, were composed of six bedrooms and one bathroom. Another rather large room on the second floor was the morning room. Facing west with a beautiful view

John Evans II, the grandson of Territorial Governor John Evans, married his high school sweetheart, Gladys Cheesman, in 1908. Following the death of Mrs. Alice Cheesman in 1923, Evans became the second owner of the historic mansion. *Denver Public Library.*

of the mountains, this was a private family gathering place. The third floor contained rooms for the servants and additional rooms for guests. In all, the mansion contained twenty-seven rooms.

Over the years, Mrs. Cheesman added personal touches to her home, including paintings, European pieces of carved jade or quartz and bronze statues. Her personal favorite was a clock and candelabra of ormolu and alabaster, a gift from her granddaughter, which she placed prominently on the fireplace mantle in the informal family room.

Shortly after Mrs. Cheesman and her daughter, Gladys, moved into the stately home, Gladys married her childhood sweetheart, John Evans II, on November 8, 1908. Evans was the grandson of Colorado's second territorial governor. The newlyweds shared the house with Mrs. Cheesman for several years. During their time in the mansion, Gladys and John Evans added unique features, including a rose garden featuring a large fountain and a lily pool with floating pergola. Broad stone steps led from the garden down to the terrace, which featured trees, flowers and shrubs, graced with carved European cherubs. The only addition the Cheesman family made to their mansion was the expansion of the sunroom in 1915.

When Mrs. Alice Cheesman died in 1923, her daughter, Gladys, put the mansion up for sale. She and her husband then moved into their own newly completed Denver home.

And the Rest Is History

Not long after the mansion was listed for sale, Claude K. Boettcher bought the property for $75,000 and, in a loving gesture, gave the deed to his wife, Edna, as a Valentine's Day present in 1924. Members of the Boettcher family, like the Cheesmans, were also pioneers in Colorado and instrumental in the establishment and growth of the state.

Claude K. Boettcher, the son of Charles and Fannie Boettcher, worked with his father in many of the businesses in the family's financial empire that included sugar, livestock, cement, steel, securities, utilities and transportation. Yet he became very successful in various enterprises in his own right. In 1897, at the age of twenty-two, Claude had received his degree in engineering from Harvard University. He later became affiliated with the powerful Colorado Fuel and Iron Company and eventually became the director. Other business ventures included the Big Horn Cattle Company, the Denver Intermountain

Railway and the Denver Tramway Corporation. Thus, he had tremendous power and influence, and he loved to entertain.

In 1900, Claude married De Allan McMurtry, the daughter of John McMurtry, a wealthy Kansas businessman. The couple had one child, Charles Boettcher II. The marriage ultimately ended in divorce. Claude remarried in 1920. His bride, Edna Case McIlvaine, who was also divorced, was the daughter of a well-known Denver physician, Austin G. Case.

Claude continued the family business tradition by including his own son in many of the family's varied interests and even joining in a few of his son's business ventures. Claude Boettcher was an avid fan of aviation and was an accomplished pilot. His son also had an interest, possibly due to his friendship with Charles Lindbergh. In any case, father and son formed the Aviation Corporation. This corporation and the Boettchers' influence helped bring in investors to eventually build the Denver Municipal Airport.

When the Boettcher family moved into the mansion, they filled their family home with unique furnishings and antiques from around the world. Among their finest possessions was a Waterford cut-crystal chandelier that was hanging in the White House during President Grant's term in 1876, when America celebrated its centennial and Colorado was admitted into the Union. The historic chandelier was hung from the center of the ground-floor drawing room, shining brightly on tapestries from France and China and a pair of eighteenth-century Venetian chairs. A twenty-foot-square handmade Russian tapestry, purchased from the Russian government for $50,000, graced one wall of the reception hall. In the library, Mrs. Boettcher placed one of her most prized possessions. The centerpiece of the room was a large mahogany desk, elaborately carved and detailed with rare delicate tulipwood and trimmed in copper. Commissioned by Louis XIV, the desk was built by Andre Boule, the most celebrated of French furniture makers. It was said to be one of only two in existence. The room was actually remodeled to complement the historic Louis XIV desk. Walls were covered with crosscut inlaid oak paneling, and several sweeping landscape paintings were placed in a creative way in the arches over the doorways.

The Boettchers made only one architectural change to the mansion in the thirty-four years they owned the home, yet it was a change that forever marked the elegance of the mansion. The original sunroom was enlarged for a second time. This time it was nearly doubled in area to an extravagant size, measuring sixty by seventy feet. The inviting location was accessible from nearly every room on the first floor. Floor-to-ceiling windows offered a view of the gardens and beautiful fountain and a splendid view of Pikes Peak

The third owner of the mansion, Claude K. Boettcher, and his wife are shown as they attend the theater. *Denver Public Library.*

to the southwest. Handcrafted leaded-glass windows, which were engraved with the Boettchers' family initials, allowed for a view of the south lawn.

The room was decorated in white. From the walls and the Colorado Yule marble floors to the fabulous Greek columns and Italian Carrara marble statues, furniture and lighting, including a spectacular crystal chandelier, everything was white. A white marble well was prominently placed near the original 1915 conservatory. This historic Italian piece came from Florence,

Herndon Davis's rendition of the exterior of the mansion. *Denver Public Library.*

Italy. The Boettchers were able to obtain the well from the city of Florence after five years of negotiations. Additional furnishings included white candelabra acquired from the Vatican in Rome, scrolled pedestal tables, benches, urns, white tapestries and white window shades. The many plants, flowers and palm trees were a wonderful contrast. The room was originally planned by the Boettchers to be used as a family gathering room. However, the splendor of the room and its décor soon became the scene of many social gatherings. Known as the Palm Room, the Denver newspapers often reported on the social and charitable events the Boettchers hosted in this room.

Amidst all the entertaining, business and political events the Boettchers hosted, Claude's son, Charles Boettcher II, did his share of entertaining in the family mansion as well. Two of his friends, in an ironic twist of fate, would have lasting effects on the younger Boettcher. One of his closest friends was the famed airplane pilot Captain Charles Lindbergh, who often stayed with the family. In fact one of the remodeled suites on the second floor was referred to as "Charlie's Room." The other was a young neighborhood boy by the name of Stephen McNichols, who lived a block away. He often rode his bike to the mansion and liked to visit with Boettcher.

During the Great Depression of the 1930s, as unemployment reached unprecedented numbers and homes and farms were being foreclosed on, public opinion turned against the rich and powerful. It was during this time that bootleggers ran the streets and gangsters began robbing banks. It was also a time when a wave of kidnappings for ransom occurred across the country, the most famous of which was the March 1, 1932 kidnapping of the baby son of Charles Lindbergh. The Boettcher family, one of Denver's richest, were also victims of a crime that epitomized that era.

In the wake of the Lindbergh baby abduction, many people realized that kidnapping for ransom could be profitable. One man moved to Denver and began his search for a wealthy businessman with the idea of kidnapping in mind. Verne Sankey soon worked his way into a bootlegging enterprise that counted the elite of Denver's Seventeenth Street businessmen among its best customers. With this connection, he learned of the names and addresses of several prominent businessmen. Among his list of prospects was Charles Boettcher II. Sankey began stalking Boettcher, following him as he went about his daily routine.

On a cold January night in 1933, Sankey executed his plan. At the southwest corner of Eighth Avenue and Washington Street—777 Washington Street, to be exact—Sankey and an accomplice made their move. Boettcher pulled his vehicle into the driveway. As he got out of the car, the two armed men grabbed him. Boettcher's wife, Anna Lou, who was eight months pregnant, watched in horror from the passenger seat. The men instructed her not to call the police and left the scene with Charles Boettcher II.

As soon as the terrified woman composed herself, Anna Lou immediately placed a call to her father-in-law, Claude Boettcher. The entire family, including the patriarch, eighty-year-old Charles Boettcher, gathered together at the mansion. After some discussion, the elder Boettcher phoned the Denver police department. A few days later, the family received a ransom note demanding $60,000. The note offered several clues to the identity of the kidnapper and also revealed the possibility that Boettcher had been taken across the state line. Thus, the newly formed FBI, under the direction of J. Edgar Hoover, was called in to the case. Sankey and his accomplice, Gordon Alcorn, were two of the most wanted criminals in the country. They had successfully conducted kidnappings for ransom in the past few years and were initially suspected in the Lindbergh baby kidnapping. Sankey became the first person in the history of the FBI to become Public Enemy No. 1. A nationwide manhunt was launched by the FBI.

Meanwhile, the Boettcher family took a bold step. They hired a private detective and publicly offered a reward. The news of a high-profile kidnapping and the demand for ransom soon swept the country. It was a front-page news story all across America. Newspaper reporters swarmed the mansion looking for new leads to the story. One local reporter talked a young neighborhood boy into sneaking into the mansion through a window to see what he could find out. As the boy was crawling through the window, one leg hanging outside, a shotgun was poked into his face. The man with the shotgun was "Old man Boettcher, and he told me to get out of there," the boy later recalled. That boy was Stephen McNichols. The young lad would see the inside of the mansion again, but on that day in 1933, he skedaddled.

Why the newspaper reporters went to the Boettcher mansion for a story can only be attributed to either bad investigation or sensationalism by the yellow journalism of the day. The facts were clear in the Denver police reports, available to the reporters, that the abduction of Boettcher occurred at 777 Washington Street, the residence of Mr. and Mrs. Charles Boettcher II.

While the FBI worked the case, including arresting Sankey's wife, Fern, the Boettcher family and Sankey continued their ransom negotiations. The press, learning Sankey was a suspect, accused Sankey of being involved in nearly every unsolved kidnapping in the country, including the murder of the Lindbergh baby.

Finally, after two long weeks, Sankey contacted the Boettchers again, who readily agreed to pay the ransom. Receiving the money, Sankey released the heir to the Boettcher fortune in a field some twelve miles north of Denver. Sankey was apprehended in a barbershop in Chicago, Illinois, on January 31, 1934, by local police and federal agents. He was extradited back to South Dakota, where he had held Boettcher captive for those two horrific weeks.

Time Magazine ran a full-length article in its March 13, 1933 issue. Titled "CRIME: Unusual Victim," the piece had many inaccuracies typical of the sensational journalism of the day, not to mention shoddy investigation. The first paragraph is enough of an example:

> *Safely home last week came Charles Boettcher II, 31, wealthy Denver investment broker who had been kidnapped on the night of Feb. 12. His story: After being carried for some 18 hr. in an automobile, he was kept with eyes taped in a room which he judged by its musty smell to be a cellar. He never saw the two, possibly three, men who guarded him. Returning, they left him on a side-street in East Denver. Commonly accepted report was that a Boettcher friend had tossed $60,000 ransom across a railroad culvert.*

The Denver newspapers had covered the story in detail since the kidnapping in early January, not February. Contrary to the "commonly accepted report," the media also reported on the return of Boettcher and printed the interviews that his father gave, stating that he did indeed pay the ransom. Nevertheless, the national media coverage proved to be too much for Sankey. He later hanged himself in his jail cell before any trial could be held.

Eventually, life got back to normal for the Boettchers. Father, son and grandson continued in their many joint businesses and soon developed new projects. Yet in the 1930s, as the Great Depression dragged on, the economy continued to weaken. Horace Bennett and Charles Boettcher had formed a partnership in 1922 when they purchased Denver's prestigious Brown Palace Hotel. However, due to the declining economy, Bennett was forced to liquidate many of his holdings. Charles and Claude Boettcher purchased Bennett's half interest in the hotel. While his father had reservations about the transaction, Claude assured him that it would prove to be a good investment.

As the Great Depression continued, World War II had its effect on the entire country, including the Boettcher family. It was also a time of unity throughout the country. The Boettcher Foundation, formed in 1937 by Claude and his father, provided needed funds to keep the hospitals operating and for the local Red Cross so it could continue its humanitarian efforts during the war.

By the 1950s, America experienced new prosperity, and entertainment at the Boettcher mansion was once again covered in the society columns of the Denver newspapers. Perhaps the most famous social event was a lavish party hosted in 1952 for the Boettchers' close friend General Dwight D. Eisenhower. To a large group of Denver's social elite, Boettcher offered a champagne toast to his friend, "the next president of the United States." Eisenhower was elected to the highest office later that year. The two men remained lifelong friends.

Claude Boettcher died in 1957, and his wife, Edna, died the following year. Edna Boettcher left the house to the Boettcher Foundation, headed by son Charles Boettcher II. The foundation offered the mansion to the state of Colorado to be used as the governor's residence. However, several state agencies initially rejected the gift. Thus, the fate of the mansion hung in the balance. In early 1959, the Boettcher Foundation began an inventory of the contents of the house, preparing for an auction. Because of the location of the Boettcher home, the land was deemed to be more valuable than the mansion, according to those who were advising the foundation. Plans began for the demolition of the historic mansion.

Fortunately for all concerned, and particularly the citizens of Colorado, when newspapers reported on the pending demolition of one of Denver's most historic homes, people from Denver and all over the state rallied in support of saving the mansion. As is often the case, the politicians, once aware of the public's desire, finally began to revisit the idea of a governor's residence. As the politicians argued the merits of accepting the mansion, questions were raised about the cost of maintenance and the idea of a governor living like a millionaire. In a ten-to-one vote against the acquisition, the measure was defeated by the state legislature. Undaunted, Governor Stephen McNichols, an early supporter of the acquisition, overruled the legislature. He had negotiated with a foundation, which agreed to finance maintenance of the residence. On the last day of 1959, Governor Stephen McNichols accepted the mansion on behalf of the state of Colorado. Quoted in the press, he said, "I was born a block away from the mansion and grew up at 607 Pennsylvania. I knew the block on the hill like the back of my hand. I used to take grapes and apples out of there many times as a kid."

In a twist of fate, the young neighborhood boy who had attempted to sneak into the mansion in 1933, when Charles Boettcher II had been kidnapped was none other than Stephen McNichols, now the governor of the state of Colorado. It was quite fitting that during the ceremony transferring the property to the state, Charles Boettcher II, twenty-six years after the kidnapping, personally handed the deed to Governor McNichols, his friend and former neighbor.

The mansion was in need of renovation, including fumigating, painting and remodeling. This process was slowed as the state politicians, still unhappy with the acquisition, delayed the needed appropriations for funding the renovations. In the end, Governor McNichols's steadfast resolve in preserving the mansion for all of Colorado succeeded. A little over a year later, the governor moved into the Boettcher mansion, now known as the Governor's Mansion. Years later, McNichols reflected on the experience. In a July 1983 interview with the *Denver Post*, he said, "If I had the chance, I'd do it again. The Boettcher mansion was well-built, beautiful, and supplied with works of art and everything a state needed."

Today

Thanks to the foresight of Governor McNichols, today the Colorado Governor's Residence, the former home of the Cheesman, Boettcher and Evans families, is open to the public for tours and special events. For over fifty years, this historic Denver residence has served as the governor's mansion. It has undergone three renovations, while remaining true to the history of the house and the previous owners. The executive mansion that began as a private home has become a historic landmark listed on the National Register of Historic Places.

Visitors to the home are treated to the opulence of the residence. The tour features the fabulous furniture and exquisite art with connections to the pioneer Cheesman, Evans and Boettcher families, to the modern era and the great significance of the state's most relevant residence, the home of the state's governor, the most powerful man, if only for a short time.

The rooms on the ground floor that are open to public viewing include the State Dining Room, which features the original long dining table. The library includes a Victorian glass case that displays Mrs. Alice Cheesman's collection of unusual jade sculptures. The room also contains four armchairs that date from 1690. In the drawing room, the White House crystal chandelier from Grant's presidency still hangs in its original place, as it has since the days of the Boettchers' ownership. The Tiffany clock and candelabra, also belonging to Mrs. Cheesman, grace the fireplace mantle as they have since the Cheesmans lived in the home over a century ago. This room also contains several European and Oriental objects, many of which were collected by the Boettcher family.

The historic pieces of furniture, art and many of the tapestries collected by the Boettchers are prominently displayed throughout the mansion. Of the many pieces, a few stand out, such as the Italian table inlaid with ebony and adorned with silver mountings, and a sixteenth-century hand-carved Italian credenza. Artwork from France, Italy and China grace the walls, including a 1740 Italian tapestry, one of several rare tapestries that decorate the mansion.

The second and third floors of the residence are the private living quarters of the governor and his family. The second floor received extensive remodeling in 1987, which today features the elegant guest suite considered the showpiece of the mansion's historic splendor. This three-room suite features Venetian furnishings that were in storage since the Cheesman era of ownership.

Exterior view of the Cheesman-Boettcher Mansion. *Linda Wommack.*

Originally, this was the room fondly known as "Charlie's Room," for Charles Lindbergh, during the Boettcher era. Among the treasured attic finds now on display are twin sleigh beds, an armoire, a desk and a crystal chandelier.

While the landscaping of the mansion's grounds has evolved throughout the years, many improvements were done in keeping with the original Victorian décor. Added features include a small rock garden with columns and a wide Italian balustrade around the upper terrace of the gardens. Stone benches allow the visitor to sit and take in the view of the beautiful setting. The trees that were planted by the Cheesmans still stand today. Tall and strong, offering shade as originally intended, the trees add a fitting natural grace to the home of Colorado pioneers and the executive leader of the state.

Fun Facts

- A portion of the Cheesmans' land between Broadway and Lincoln Street and Sixteenth Street and Colfax Avenue was used as a cow pasture. The family's favorite cow, Betsy, occasionally drew complaints from the neighbors.
- Following the death of Walter Cheesman, his widow lobbied the city of Denver to name the new city park, the former city cemetery, in honor of her husband. Chessman Park is graced by a fine Colorado marble pavilion paid for by Mrs. Cheesman.
- Legend has it that the popular Palm Room was decorated in white because Mrs. Edna Boettcher believed that white complemented her looks.
- The new government agency, the Federal Bureau of Investigation, headed by J. Edgar Hoover, began its infamous "Public Enemy" list during this era. Verne Sankey was the first man to be known across the country as Public Enemy No. 1. After his quick capture, the FBI turned their sights on the gangsters. The next Public Enemy No. 1 was none other than John Dillinger.
- The Boettcher family owned the Brown Palace from 1922 until 1980, the last of the owners with Colorado ties. Claude Boettcher had a suite at the hotel where he often stayed and later lived in his twilight years. In the evenings, he enjoyed a cold Coca-Cola. However, he would walk across the street to the drugstore to purchase his beverage because the hotel price was too high.
- The Cheesman-Boettcher Mansion (Governor's Mansion) was placed on the National Register on December 3, 1969, 5DV.169.

Contact Information

GOVERNOR'S RESIDENCE AT THE BOETTCHER MANSION
400 East Eighth Avenue
Denver, Colorado 80203
www.Coloradogov.org
(303) 866-5344

BIBLIOGRAPHY

Books

Appleby, Susan Consola. *Fading Past: The Story of Douglas County, Colorado.* Palmer Lake, CO: Filter Press, LLC, 2001.

Athearn, Robert G. *Rebel of the Rockies: A History of the Denver and Rio Grande Western Railroad.* New Haven, CT: Yale University Press, 1962.

Bean, Geraldine. *Charles Boettcher: A Study in Pioneer Western Enterprise.* Boulder, CO: Westview Press, 1976.

Bjorkman, Timothy W. *Verne Sankey: America's First Public Enemy.* Oklahoma City: University of Oklahoma Press, 2007.

Blair, Edward. *Leadville: Colorado's Magic City.* Boulder, CO: Pruett Publishing, 1980.

Bretz, James. *Mansions of Denver: The Vintage Years, 1870–1938.* Boulder, CO: Pruett Publishing, 2005.

Brown, Georgina. *A Look at Leadville's Homes of Fortune.* Leadville, CO: B&B Printers, 1976.

Brown, Robert L. *Ghost Towns of the Colorado Rockies* Caldwell, ID: Caxton Press, 1982.

Brown, Ronald. *Hard-Rock Miners: The Intermountain West, 1860–1920.* College Station: Texas A&M University Press, 1979.

Burns, Ken, Ric Burns and Geoffrey C. Ward. *The Civil War: An Illustrated History.* New York: Alfred A. Knopf, Inc. 1990.

Byers, William N. *Hand Book to the Gold Fields of Nebraska and Kansas*. Chicago: D.B. Cooke of Chicago, 1859.

Catlett, Sharon R. *Farmlands, Forts, and Country Life: The Story Of Southwest Denver*. Boulder, CO: Big Earth Publishing, 2007.

Davis, Sally, and Betty Baldwin. *Denver Dwellings and Descendants*. Denver, CO: Sage Books, 1963.

Dodds, Joanne West. *The Thatchers: Hard Work Won the West*. Pueblo, CO: My Friend the Printer, Inc., 2001.

Eberhart, Perry. *Ghosts of the Colorado Plains*. Denver, CO: Sage Books, 1986.
———. *Guide to Ghost Towns and Mining Camps*. Denver, CO: Sage Books, 1959.

Fetler, John. *The Pikes Peak People*. Caldwell, ID: Caxton Press, 1966.

Griswold, Don L., and Jean Harvey Griswold. *History of Leadville and Lake County, Colorado*. Denver: Colorado Historical Society, 1996.

Hafen, Leroy. *Pikes Peak Gold Rush Guidebooks of 1859*. Glendale, CA: Arthur Clark Publishers, 1941.

Haley, J. Evetts. *Charles Goodnight: Cowman and Plainsman*. Oklahoma: University of Oklahoma Press, 1936.

Hall, Frank. *History of the State of Colorado*. Volumes I through IV. Chicago: Blakely Printing Company of Chicago, 1889.

Higgins, Rachel, and Peggie Yager. *Memoirs of Miramont Castle*. Manitou Springs, CO: Manitou Springs Historical Society, 2012.

Iversen, Kristen. *Molly Brown: Unraveling the Truth*. Boulder, CO: Johnson Books, 1999.

Lohse, Joyce B. *Unsinkable: The Molly Brown Story*. Palmer Lake, CO: Filter Press, LLC, 2006.

Marr, Josephine Lowell. *Douglas County: A Historical Journey*. Gunnison, CO: B&B Printers, 1983.

Mathews, Frances, and Kay Stillman. *Rosemount Museum: A Pictorial Guide*. Pueblo, CO: Rosemount Museum Association, 1985.

Noel, Thomas J. *Buildings of Colorado*. New York: Oxford University Press, 1997.
———. *Colorado Catholicism*. Boulder: University Press of Colorado, 1989.

Perkins, Robert L. *The First Hundred Years*. Garden City, NY: Doubleday & Company Publishers, 1959.

Pulcipher, Robert S. *The Pioneer Western Bank: First of Denver, 1860–1980*. Denver, CO: First Interstate Bank of Denver and Robert S. Pulcipher, publishers, 1984.

Royem, Robert T. *America's Railroad: The Official Guidebook of the Durango & Silverton Narrow Gauge Railroad*. Durango, CO: The Durango & Silverton Narrow Gauge Railroad, 2007.

Sifakis, Stewart. *Who Was Who in the Civil War*. New York: Facts On File, Inc., 1988.

Smith, Duane A. *Durango Diary*. Durango, CO: The Herald Press, 1996.

————. *Rocky Mountain Mining Camps*. Boulder: University Press of Colorado, 1992.

Smith, Duane A., and Richard D. Lamm. *Pioneers & Politicians: 10 Colorado Governors in Profile*. Boulder, CO: Pruett Publishing, 1984.

Van Cise, Philip. *Fighting the Underworld*. Boston: Houghton Mifflin Company, 1936.

Von Bamford, Lawrence. *Leadville Architecture: A Legacy of Silver: 1860–1899*. Estes Park, CO: Architecture Research Press, 1996.

Werner, Patricia. *The Walls Talk: Historic House Museums of Colorado*. Palmer Lake, CO: Filter Press, LLC, 2010.

Whitacre, Christine. *Molly Brown: Denver's Unsinkable Lady*. Denver, CO: Historic Denver Inc., 1984.

Wommack, Linda. *Colorado's Landmark Hotels*. Palmer Lake, CO: Filter Press, LLC, 2012.

————. *From the Grave*. Caldwell, ID: Caxton Press, 1998.

Voynick, Stephen M. *Leadville: A Miners' Epic*. Missoula, MT: Mountain Press Publishing Company, 1984.

Zamonski, Stanley W., and Teddy Kelle. *The '59ers*. Frederick, CO: Platte 'N Press Books, 1961.

Colorado History Center

James B. Grant Collection, 1848–1911.

Office of Archaeology & Historic Preservation, including city and county preservation records.

National Register of County and State records of the State Historic Preservation Office.

William J. Palmer Collection, including papers, letters and documents.

William N. Byers Papers.

Denver Public Library Western History Collection

Frank Bloom, Remembrances, Trinidad, Colorado. Collection #M1589. Photos courtesy Coi Gerhig, DPL photo editor.

Additional Sources

Connie Clayton, genealogist consultant, Fraser, Colorado. Research including birth and death dates, documents and census records.
Douglas County Genealogical Society.
Miramont Castle Museum archives, courtesy Peggie Yager.
Molly Brown House Museum archives.
Rosemount Victorian House archives.
Trinidad History Museum, Colorado History Center. Correspondence letters between Sarah Thatcher and Frank Bloom.

Interviews and Correspondence

Heather Bryson, owner, Gable House. April 11, June 26 and 27 and July 28 and 29, 2014.
Maretta Characky, Robison Mansion historian. April 2, 9 and 17, 2013; May 17 and 24, 2014; June 6 and 7, 2014; July 16 and 17, 2014.
Melissa Feher-Peiker, owner, Castle Marne. May 10, 15 and 21 and November 5, 2013.
James "Jim" Peiker, owner, Castle Marne. November 5 and December 3, 2013; January 6, 7, 8, 9 and 10, 2014.
Robert Pulcipher, First National Bank historian, November 10, 2012; January 8 and June 18, 19 and 20, 2013; January 27, 28, 29 and 30, 2014; and Februrary 1, 2014.

Maureen Scanlon, director of the Healy House Museum and Dexter Cabin, Leadville. September 21, 23, 25 and 30, 2013; October 13, 2013; and December 2, 7, 21, 22 and 23, 2013.

Peggie Yager, curator, Miramont Castle Museum. June 26, 2013; July 5, 8 and 9, 2013.

Newspapers

The various local newspaper archives accessed for this work are noted in the exact quotes used throughout the text. Additional information is attributed to the following publication:

Cannon, Helen. "First Ladies of Colorado: Mary Goodell Grant," *Colorado Magazine*, Winter 1964.

INDEX

ABOUT THE AUTHOR

A Colorado native, Linda Wommack is a Colorado historian and historical consultant. She has written seven books on Colorado history, including *Colorado's Landmark Hotels*, *From the Grave: Colorado's Pioneer Cemeteries*, *Our Ladies of the Tenderloin: Colorado's Legends in Lace* and *Colorado History for Kids*. She has also contributed to two anthologies concerning Western Americana.

Linda has been a contributing editor for *True West Magazine* since 1995. She has also been a staff writer, contributing a monthly article for *Wild West Magazine*, since 2004. She has also written for the *Tombstone Epitaph*, the nation's oldest continuously published newspaper, since 1993. Linda also writes for several publications throughout her state.

Linda's research has been used in several documentary accounts for the national Wild West History Association and historical treatises of the Sand Creek Massacre, as well as critical historic aspects for the new Lawman & Outlaw Museum in Cripple Creek, Colorado, which opened in 2007.

Linda feeds her passion for history with activities in many local, state and national preservation projects; participating in historical venues, including speaking engagements and hosting tours; and is involved in historical reenactments across the state.

As a longtime member of the national Western Writers of America, she has served as a judge for the acclaimed national Spur Awards in Western Americana literature for eight years. She is a member of both the state and national Cemetery Preservation Associations, the Gilpin County Historical Society and the national Wild West History Association and is an honorary lifetime member of the Pikes Peak Heritage Society. As a member of Women Writing the West (WWW), Linda has organized quarterly meetings for the Colorado members of WWW for the past six years and served on the 2014 WWW Convention Steering Committee.